JAN   2010

W9-ACR-631

Heritage Edition

The Pawnee

Indians of North America

Heritage Edition

Indians
of North
America

Heritage Edition

Indians of North America

The Pawnee

Theresa Jensen Lacey

Foreword by
Ada E. Deer
University of Wisconsin–Madison

CHELSEA HOUSE
PUBLISHERS
An imprint of Infobase Publishing

THE PAWNEE

Copyright © 2006 by Infobase Publishing

Chelsea House
An imprint of Infobase Publishing
132 West 31st Street
New York, NY 10001

Library of Congress Cataloging-in-Publication Data

Lacey, Theresa Jensen.
  The Pawnee / Theresa Jensen Lacey.
     p. cm. — (Indians of North America)
  Includes index.
  ISBN 0-7910-8599-6 (hard cover)
  1. Pawnee Indians—History—Juvenile literature. 2. Pawnee Indians—Social life and customs—Juvenile literature. I. Title. II. Indians of North America (Chelsea House Publishers)
  E99.P3L33 2005
  978.004'97933—dc22

                                                                2005006512

Chelsea House books are available at special discounts when purchased in bulk quantities for businesses, associations, institutions, or sales promotions. Please call our Special Sales Department in New York at (212) 967-8800 or (800) 322-8755.

You can find Chelsea House on the World Wide Web at
http://www.chelseahouse.com

Series and cover design by Keith Trego

Printed in the United States of America

9 8 7 6 5 4 3 2

Contents

Foreword

Ada E. Deer

American Indians are an integral part of our nation's life and history. Yet most Americans think of their Indian neighbors as stereotypes; they are woefully uninformed about them as fellow humans. They know little about the history, culture, and contributions of Native people. In this new millennium, it is essential for every American to know, understand, and share in our common heritage. The Cherokee teacher, the Mohawk steelworker, and the Ojibwe writer all express their tribal heritage while living in mainstream America.

The revised INDIANS OF NORTH AMERICA series, which focuses on some of the continent's larger tribes, provides the reader with an accurate perspective that will better equip him/her to live and work in today's world. Each tribe has a unique history and culture, and knowledge of individual tribes is essential to understanding the Indian experience.

Prior to the arrival of Columbus in 1492, scholars estimate the Native population north of the Rio Grande ranged from seven to twenty-five million people who spoke more than three hundred different languages. It has been estimated that ninety percent of the Native population was wiped out by disease, war, relocation, and starvation. Today there are more than 567 tribes, which have a total population of more than two million. When Columbus arrived in the Bahamas, the Arawak Indians greeted him with gifts, friendship, and hospitality. He noted their ignorance of guns and swords and wrote they could easily be overtaken with fifty men and made to do whatever he wished. This unresolved clash in perspectives continues to this day.

A holistic view recognizing the connections of all people, the land, and animals pervades the life and thinking of Native people. These core values—respect for each other and all living things; honoring the elders; caring, sharing, and living in balance with nature; and using not abusing the land and its resources—have sustained Native people for thousands of years.

American Indians are recognized in the U.S. Constitution. They are the only group in this country who has a distinctive *political* relationship with the federal government. This relationship is based on the U.S. Constitution, treaties, court decisions, and attorney-general opinions. Through the treaty process, millions of acres of land were ceded *to* the U.S. government *by* the tribes. In return, the United States agreed to provide protection, health care, education, and other services. All 377 treaties were broken by the United States. Yet treaties are the supreme law of the land as stated in the U.S. Constitution and are still valid. Treaties made more than one hundred years ago uphold tribal rights to hunt, fish, and gather.

Since 1778, when the first treaty was signed with the Lenni-Lenape, tribal sovereignty has been recognized and a government-to-government relationship was established. This concept of tribal power and authority has continuously been misunderstood by the general public and undermined by the states. In a series of court decisions in the 1830s, Chief Justice John Marshall described tribes as "domestic dependent nations." This status is not easily understood by most people and is rejected by state governments who often ignore and/or challenge tribal sovereignty. Sadly, many individual Indians and tribal governments do not understand the powers and limitations of tribal sovereignty. An overarching fact is that Congress has plenary, or absolute, power over Indians and can exercise this sweeping power at any time. Thus, sovereignty is tenuous.

Since the July 8, 1970, message President Richard Nixon issued to Congress in which he emphasized "self-determination without termination," tribes have re-emerged and have utilized the opportunities presented by the passage of major legislation such as the American Indian Tribal College Act (1971), Indian Education Act (1972), Indian Education and Self-Determination Act (1975), American Indian Health Care Improvement Act (1976), Indian Child Welfare Act (1978), American Indian Religious Freedom Act (1978), Indian Gaming Regulatory Act (1988), and Native American Graves Preservation and Repatriation Act (1990). Each of these laws has enabled tribes to exercise many facets of their sovereignty and consequently has resulted in many clashes and controversies with the states and the general public. However, tribes now have more access to and can afford attorneys to protect their rights and assets.

Under provisions of these laws, many Indian tribes reclaimed power over their children's education with the establishment of tribal schools and thirty-one tribal colleges. Many Indian children have been rescued from the foster-care system. More tribal people are freely practicing their traditional religions. Tribes with gaming revenue have raised their standard of living with improved housing, schools, health clinics, and other benefits. Ancestors' bones have been reclaimed and properly buried. All of these laws affect and involve the federal, state, and local governments as well as individual citizens.

Tribes are no longer people of the past. They are major players in today's economic and political arenas; contributing millions of dollars to the states under the gaming compacts and supporting political candidates. Each of the tribes in INDIANS OF NORTH AMERICA demonstrates remarkable endurance, strength, and adaptability. They are buying land, teaching their language and culture, and creating and expanding their economic base, while developing their people and making decisions for future generations. Tribes will continue to exist, survive, and thrive.

Ada E. Deer
University of Wisconsin–Madison
June 2004

1

Origins of the Pawnees

The prairie lands in which the Pawnees settled, known to the European immigrants as Nebraska Territory, was one from which the First People had a grand view of the night skies. It was thus natural for their beliefs in the beginnings of life to be focused upon the stars. The stars and celestial bodies provided the Pawnees with a basis for their religion, directed their lives, and fueled their imaginations. The stars also served as inspiration for their creation myth.

The Pawnee people referred to their god, from which all life sprang, as *Atius Tirawa*, or *Tirawahat*, or simply *Tirawa*, which means "The Expanse of the Heavens." The Pawnees say that there was always Tirawa; in the beginning, there was only Tirawa. Tirawa lived in the heavens. He was alone, and wanted something or someone else for company. But before he did anything about it, he stopped to think about what he wanted to do.

It is important to note that thought before action is intrinsic to

This oil rendition of Ah-sháw-wah-róoks-te, or Medicine Horse, was painted by renowned frontier artist George Catlin and is on display at the Smithsonian American Art Museum in Washington, D.C. In 1832, Catlin traveled up the Missouri River, where he visited eighteen tribes, including the Pawnee, who lived on the prairie lands of present-day Kansas and Nebraska.

the Pawnee philosophy of life. To the Pawnees, there can be nothing without there first being thought. The thinking individual was the very essence of humanity, the connection with the Great Mind.

Therefore the process of creation began with Tirawa having

thoughts about it. He decided he would like to have a universe and stars, and so created the first ones, placing them in the four cardinal directions. The Evening Star was placed in the west; she was given the moon to help her. In the east, Tirawa placed the Morning Star; he was given the sun as his helper. In the other two cardinal directions he placed the North Star and the South Star. Tirawa also placed four stars in the semi-cardinal directions (the northeast, northwest, southeast, and south-west), and told them that they were to hold the heavens up for all eternity.

The stars in the four cardinal directions were given the power to create the earth. Tirawa gave the Evening Star tools with which to do this. She was given all the ingredients neces-sary to make life-giving storms: wind, clouds, lightning, and thunder.

Evening Star caused the first storm. With one great flash of lightning, a loud clap of thunder, and a fierce wind, the earth was created; but there was no life on it or in it. Tirawa told the Evening Star to sing; when she did, the face of the earth became covered with water.

Tirawa told the stars in the four semi-cardinal directions to strike the earth with war clubs made of hemlock. When they did, the waters parted; dry land and mountains appeared. Another storm came, the wind blew, the rain fell hard upon the earth, and lightning struck the ground. The lightning made the earth fertile and able to sustain life. Thunder shook the ground; as it settled from the shaking, the earth formed mountains and valleys. Another storm came, and the forests and other fauna were created. A fourth storm caused rains to come to earth, fill-ing the shallow places of the land with sweet, fresh water.

The star-gods then dropped seeds upon the earth. The seeds sprouted and became living plants. After this, Tirawa rested for a time.

Tirawa told the stars, "Take human form; make people on the earth in that image." But in a council with the other stars,

Morning Star and Evening Star quarreled. Morning Star was in love with Evening Star and knew that they should have children. Morning Star said that having children with Evening Star was the only way the earth would ever have people on it, and he was determined to have Evening Star as his wife. Up in the sky, knowing that Morning Star was coming for her, Evening Star put four fierce animals in the semi-cardinal directions. She put a wolf in the southeast and gave him the power of clouds. In the southwest, Evening Star placed a wildcat, which had the power of the winds. She placed a mountain lion in the northwest, and gave him the power of lightning. In the northeast, Evening Star placed a bear with the power of thunder. She said, "When Morning Star comes, you are all to attack him."

Before Morning Star came, other stars tried to court Evening Star; she had her animals dispatch them all. But Morning Star had help in the form of the Sun. When finally Morning Star and the Sun came for her, Evening Star and her guard animals had been fighting off all other would-be suitors. Seeing Morning Star with the Sun, Evening Star and her guard animals were taken aback. She said, "You have been brave and determined. I believe you are worthy of me now." Evening Star agreed to marry Morning Star. Together they made the very first human being, a female child. She was carried from heaven to earth by a whirlwind. Later, Evening Star and Morning Star had another child, a male. He was also sent to Earth.

The population of the earth increased over time. Evening Star instructed the females in the care of the earth's gifts, how to make a tepee and an *earth lodge*, and how to care for children. Morning Star taught the male children how to protect themselves and their families, how to hunt, and how to travel over the earth. Morning Star gave the male children their warrior's clothing. Evening Star came many times to see how her children fared, and she taught the people sacred songs and the stories of creation so that they would always remember how they came to Earth and to be grateful for their creation.

After a while, the people went out hunting, farther and farther from their camp, until they came upon other people; then they knew that they were not the only ones on earth. There were many people on the face of the earth, much like themselves, only a little different.

The first boy child made by Morning Star and Evening Star grew up and was called First Man. After discovering these other villages, First Man sent messengers to them, inviting them to a great council. He moved his village to a more centralized location, so it would be convenient for all of the people to meet. This village became known as Center Village; First Man was called Chief of Center Village.

The people of the other villages came to the council, bearing gifts and buffalo meat. So that each village would know it had equal responsibilities toward the people and could enjoy as much regard as any other, Chief of Center Village created different *medicine bundles*, or a collection of sacred things, for each of them. With the help of Evening Star and Morning Star, Chief of Center Village and all the people developed their ceremonies, symbols, and special songs. It was then that the people banded together to form a nation, bound with the spiritual gifts they shared.

Establishing ceremonies gave order to the cycles of Pawnee life and coordinated their actions, giving meaning to the smallest things they did. Even today, in the cycle of seasonal ceremonies, the people use medicine bundles. There is an Evening Star bundle, representing the creation; a Morning Star bundle; bundles representing the four semi-cardinal directions; and the Skull bundle, which represents intellectual creativity, especially as it came from First Man.

Many of the beliefs in the legends and old stories of the Pawnees focused upon the stars and the animals that were part of their environment. One of the animals that figures prominently in legend is the sandhill crane. Every spring for thousands of years, sandhill cranes have come in great numbers to

By the time the Spanish began to explore the southern portion of Pawnee territory in the mid-sixteenth century, the Pawnees had largely settled along the Platte River, where they grew crops such as corn, beans, and squash. The Pawnees generally lived in earthen lodges, but did use tepees for shelter when they hunted buffalo.

the sandbars of the Platte River. Here they rest and feed on marsh tubers and small reptiles, gaining strength and weight for the long flight to their Arctic nesting grounds. Seeing these birds every spring, the Pawnees were both mystified and fascinated by them, with their large bodies, long necks, and loud, trumpeting calls. There are some stories in which the cranes cause mischief and bring trouble for the people; the following is such a story.

One very hot summer night, many of the people came out of their tepees to sleep under the open sky, with the cool breezes and the sweet smell of the prairie grasses blowing over them. Among them was a young girl named Feather Woman. Just before dawn, Feather Woman awoke suddenly and looked up into the sky, which was still dark. She watched the bright Morning Star as it rose and was fascinated. Feather Woman whispered, "Morning Star, I love you! If I could find a husband who is as beautiful as you, I would be happy." She watched the Morning Star until it faded with the rising of the sun.

That summer, Feather Woman and her people were very busy. The buffalo were plentiful; many had been brought down in the hunt. There was much to be done: animals to skin, meat to cook and preserve, clothing and tools to craft. With so much to occupy her, Feather Woman had little time to think about the Morning Star.

Then, one fall afternoon, Feather Woman went out to look for firewood. So intent was she on her work, she wandered far from her people. After a time she sensed someone watching her. Turning, she gazed upon a very tall, handsome young warrior she had never seen before. The stranger was dressed in a soft white buckskin robe, beautifully embroidered and decorated with dyed porcupine quills. In his hair he wore eagle feathers; in his hand he carried a small juniper bush decorated with cobwebs.

Apprehensive, Feather Woman started to run away. The stranger caught her arm and whispered, "Feather Woman! I am Morning Star! One night last summer, I looked down; I saw you lying there in the prairie grasses, waking up beside your tepee. I fell in love with you. I heard you say that you loved me. Forget your people and come with me now! I will take you to my country, the land of the Star People."

Feather Woman hesitated, but only for an instant. She nodded, and Morning Star laid the juniper bush on the ground. He said, "Put your feet on the lowest strand of cobwebs and close your eyes." With this, Feather Woman was swept up into the sky. She opened her eyes in Star Country, with Morning Star by her side. She discovered that Star Country was much like her own, with grassy plains, hills, and lodges. Morning Star explained, "Spider Man weaves the cobwebs; we use them as ladders to come down to Earth and then to return again to the sky." He then took Feather Woman to his own lodge, also the home of his parents, Sun and Moon.

Sun was out, but Moon was at home. She was very kind to Feather Woman, but she took her son aside and said, "Morning Star, your father will not like this marriage. He does not trust Earth people. Tell Feather Woman to be wary of this, because if she disobeys any of our laws, Sun will banish her from Star Country."

Just as Moon had said, when Sun came to the lodge that night, he was indeed unhappy to meet the wife Morning Star had chosen. Sun said, "Earth people are weak and stupid. They can't be trusted." But then he said to Feather Woman, "If you obey our laws and learn our way of life, you can stay and you will be happy."

Some seasons later, Feather Woman had a child. Morning Star named him Star Boy. They were all very happy, until one day when Feather Woman went with Moon to get roots and berries. In their wanderings, they came upon a huge turnip, larger than any Feather Woman had ever seen before. The green leaves were almost as tall as she was, and the turnip was only half-buried in the earth. She was tempted to dig it up, for what a great meal it would make.

Moon said, "I see you looking at that turnip, Feather Woman. It is sacred to the Star People. Underneath the turnip lies a secret we are forbidden to know. Whoever tries to disturb this turnip will bring great sadness upon themselves. Never touch it!" Several days passed, and whenever Moon and Feather Woman would be out digging for roots or gathering firewood, they would pass the turnip. Feather Woman's digging stick itched in her hand, but she did not want to anger Moon and so refrained from giving in to temptation.

One day, however, Moon said to Feather Woman, "I must stay here in our lodge today; I feel unwell. You go on without me." And so she did. After a while, her gathering brought her close to where the great turnip lay. She said to herself, "No one will know. I will only uproot it a little and see what lies underneath, and then bury it again." She began to dig; as she did, two cranes swooped down from the sky and said to her, "We will help you uproot that turnip with our beaks!" Feather Woman was glad for their help; she did not know that the cranes were enemies of the Star People.

The cranes smiled maliciously as they flew away, leaving the great turnip uprooted and lying on its side. "There!" they called out to Feather Woman. "Now see what lies beneath!" Trumpeting loudly, they flew away. There was a huge crater where the turnip had been. Feather Woman looked down into it and far below she could see her former home. She saw some of her friends gathering berries on a hillside, and some of the warriors gathered around a fine horse one of them had just brought to camp. Feather Woman saw the children beside the fires, and the women shooing them away as they cooked. And suddenly, she was overwhelmed with a feeling of great longing for her former home and for her people.

Feather Woman watched her people through the crater, until she realized that darkness was falling. She rolled the turnip back to its place and tried to rebury it as best she could. It had been dark for a long time when she returned to her lodge; she had been missed. Once there, Sun saw her face and said, "Feather Woman, you look sad and also guilty, as if you have done something wrong. Tell me what it is!" Then Feather Woman told Sun what she had done.

"I knew that we could not trust Earth people," Sun said to Moon and Morning Star. To Feather Woman he said, "You have betrayed our trust and disturbed something that is sacred to us. You must be banished, and you will go back to the earth-home you so much long for."

Morning Star led Feather Woman and her son, Star Boy, to the place where Spider Man wove his cobwebs. Morning Star wrapped them in a white buckskin robe. Spider Man tied her with his cobwebs and led her down from the sky. As she came down, her Earth people looked up in the heavens, saying, "Look! It is a great falling star!" They watched its brightness all the way to Earth. Then they went to look for the star, to see where it had fallen. There they found Star Boy and Feather Woman, wrapped in the white robe. They were unhurt. The people took Feather Woman and Star Boy back to their camp, for they remembered her from former days.

But Feather Woman never stopped grieving for her love, the Morning Star. Every night, she would climb the highest hill and watch the skies until Morning Star appeared. She would call out, "Morning Star! Please take me back with you!" And he would respond, "You betrayed our trust; you can never return." And he would go on his way across the sky. Feather Woman finally died of a broken heart. Morning Star can still be seen each clear dawn, crossing the sky, alone.

Another popular Pawnee myth is the legend of Bear-Man. One day a young warrior on a horse raid saw a female bear cub alone in the forest. The cub looked so defenseless and small that the brave was moved with sympathy for her. He took the cub in his arms and said, "I know that our Great Spirit, Tirawa, will care for you; but I will tie a string of tobacco around your neck, to show you that I, too, care." With that, he gently knotted a tobacco string around the cub's neck and put her down again.

Once back in his lodge, the young man told his wife, who was soon to have a baby, about the bear cub. She thought so much about this bear cub that when their child was born, he looked much like a cub himself.

As the child grew older, he became more and more like a bear, both in his looks and in his ways. Even as the boy played with his friends, he would tell them, "I can turn myself into a real bear whenever I want to." They, of course, did not believe him. Still, the young boy was given a certain amount of respect by his people, for among the Pawnees the bear is considered to be the wisest of all animals.

As the boy grew older, he was asked to accompany war and raiding parties, to lend his wisdom to them. One fateful day, however, when he was with more than forty Pawnee warriors, they were set upon by a large *band* of *Sioux*, a tribe that was considered to be one of the Pawnees' greatest enemies. The Sioux killed the Pawnees, including Bear-Man, and took their scalps. Shortly afterward, some bears wandered by the ravine where the ambush had happened. A she-bear recognized Bear-Man as the child of the kind man who had blessed her with his tobacco string, long ago; she implored mercy of her friends, saying, "Let us use our medicine to make Bear-Man live again." And so together they sang the special songs and used the healing herbs about which they all knew. After a time, Bear-Man began to stir with life once more.

When Bear-Man became conscious, the bears took him to their den to fully recover and told him what they had done. As he healed, the bears taught Bear-Man even more about good medicines and all the other wise things they knew. They said, "When you use these powers, thank not ourselves, nor think that you do this by your own powers; instead, in all things give thanks to Tirawa, who made us and gave us our wisdom." They told Bear-Man, "You must go back to your people now, with all you have learned. The *cedar* tree shall be a protector to you in all that you do, because it never ages. If, during one of Tirawa's thunderstorms, you throw some cedar wood upon your fire, it will keep you safe." The bears blessed Bear-Man with their wisdom, greatness, and fearlessness.

Bear-Man returned to his people, teaching them all that the bears had taught him. He became the greatest warrior of his tribe; he was fearless, wise, and great, just as the bears had said. Bear-Man lived long ago, but such was his influence with his people that there is a special dance they made in his memory. It is called the Bear Dance, and the Pawnees still dance the Bear

This engraving of a Pawnee village along the Platte River was drawn by artist George Catlin and shows the type of dwelling the Pawnees lived in during much of the year—the earth lodge. These semi-subterranean circular lodges contained four posts that held up a series of rafters, all of which was covered by earth.

Dance and remember their source of wisdom, fearlessness, and greatness.

Mythology aside, historical accounts of the origin of the Pawnee refer to their ancestors, the *Caddoans*. The Caddoan peoples' history has been dated to prehistoric times. These tribes included the Wichita, the Arikara, the Caddo, and the Pawnee. Besides sharing linguistic similarities, these tribes also had similar lifestyles, hunting and cultivation methods, and types of dwelling.

There are a number of theories of how the Caddoans came to be on the North American continent. A four-tribal-origin theory has been borne out by researchers and geneticists, who have identified four distinct DNA strains from the various tribes and hypothetically traced the migratory paths of each. Other anthropologists say that some Native American peoples came to this continent by ocean passage.

Although no one can say for certain, the most popular and commonly accepted theory is that all Native American peoples traveled to this continent from Asia more than forty thousand years ago, utilizing a small strip of treeless land then in existence, a "land bridge" joining the two continents at the juncture of Siberia and Alaska, at the site of what is now known as the Bering Strait.

Further evidence in support of this theory was provided in 1991 by a study conducted by a biochemist named Douglas C. Wallace at Emory University in Atlanta, Georgia. Wallace took blood samples from ninety-nine different people from three geographically disparate groups of Indians: the Ticunas of South America, the Mayas of Central America, and the Pimas of North America. Wallace detected rare chemical sequences in the mitochondrial DNA of the samples and found that these sequences occurred only in the DNA of Asian populations. The obvious conclusion is that the Indians occupying the Americas originally came from Asia. Wallace did not find this chemical sequence in Eskimos, Navajos, Aleuts, and other Native groups who, he theorized, arrived here at a later time. Wallace also claimed that he was able to trace the DNA lineages of these tribes to at least four women in an early migrating group, and similar studies published as recently as 2004 have confirmed Wallace's original findings.

On the basis of this shared mitochondrial DNA, Wallace theorized that the Bering Strait trek first occurred 15,000 to 30,000 years ago. There are conflicting hypotheses, however. Geneticist Svante Paabo of the University of California–Berkeley, recently argued against some of Wallace's findings. Paabo claimed that the tribes of the Pacific Northwest have thirty, rather than four, different mitochondrial DNA sequences in common, which would place the crossing of the

Bering Strait at a much earlier date, 40,000 to 50,000 years ago. Whenever they arrived, the predecessors of present-day Native Americans began settling in and multiplying on the continent that is now North America.

The Caddoans, the ancestors of the Pawnees, lived and prospered in the fertile lands west of the Mississippi River. As time passed and tribal populations grew, they began traveling farther away in search of game. Their travels took them to the territory that is now Nebraska and Kansas.

These lands were occupied by several Native American peoples, including the Pawnee, the Caddoan, and the Kansa Indians. It is a land of rolling hills and vast prairies, with bitterly cold weather and sudden snowstorms in winter; dry, hot days in summer; and flash floods in spring. The Kansas and Arkansas rivers, with more than one hundred tributaries, brought life-giving water to the people, as well as an abundance of game and wildlife.

The land that we now know as Nebraska must have been a beautiful sight to the early Native American people, with its undulating plains, fertile soil, rugged hills called *buttes*, and more than two thousand lakes. The majority of the Pawnee population settled along the Platte River, a tributary of the Missouri. Nebraska, like Kansas, is also a land of unpredictable and extreme weather. This environment challenged the Pawnees in their daily struggle for survival and enriched them spiritually as a people.

The lands of Kansas and Nebraska were shared by the Pawnees with neighboring tribes, some of which were friends, some trading partners, and others bitter foes. Certain neighboring tribes, such as the Blackfeet, Arapaho, Kiowa, and Apache, were in the Great Plains area as early as 500 B.C. The Pawnees migrated to the Great Plains from the southwestern part of the continent about 750 years ago, or approximately A.D. 1250.

Perhaps they settled in that area because of the lure of abundant game, especially buffalo. Another contributing factor

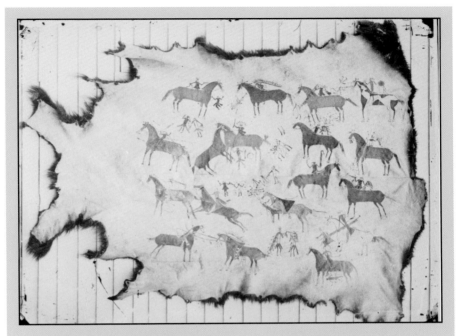

Renowned frontier photographer William Henry Jackson took this photo in 1868 of a depiction of Pawnee life on a buffalo hide. As with all Plains tribes, horses played an integral role in Pawnee life.

was trade. The Great Plains area was the connecting hub of an ancient intertribal trade route, so goods could be obtained even from tribes with whom the Pawnees were unfriendly.

The Pawnees might have traveled farther east, but soon after they arrived they encountered an influx of other tribes from the east fleeing the invasion of white settlers in their former lands. Eastern woodlands tribes such as the Sioux arrived, being forced ever westward by more and more European settlers. Ahead of the Sioux came the Cheyenne and Crow, who were also forced west. After the Plains tribes had acquired the horse from the Spanish, however, each tribe began to stand their ground and defend lands they claimed as their own.

This late-nineteenth-century photo is of a Pawnee man and woman on the plains of Nebraska. Many white settlers considered the weather and terrain of the plains unforgiving, but the Pawnees were able to thrive in this area thanks to the rich soil and seemingly endless supply of buffalo.

By the mid-eighteenth century, five principal tribes had established themselves in the area. North of where the Kansas and Missouri rivers meet was the tribe that gave Kansas its name—the Kansa, or Kaw. South of them was the Osage. Both of these tribes had come from the east. The Pawnees claimed the entire north-central portion of the Great Plains as their own, with the Wichita tribe to the south. Arriving from the eastern Rockies, the Comanches lived in what is now western Kansas.

The Great Plains area, where the Pawnee people chose to call home, ranged from the northern headwaters of the Platte River, through the Republican, Solomon, and Smoky Hill valleys, then farther south through the Great Bend of the Arkansas River.

This fantastic stretch of land experienced dramatic changes of weather. The weather could, in minutes, go from serene and balmy to wild and cold, with hail as big as a man's fist. The wind blew unremittingly, day in and day out, year in and year out, blowing hot and dry in summer, and with a ferocity that permeated the bones in winter. The vast rolling hills, the monotonous landscape unbroken by plow or well, combined with the endless whine of the wind, was enough to drive early settlers and explorers mad. But to the Pawnees it was home.

Here the Pawnees found everything they needed for survival and aesthetic satisfaction. The soil was rich and good for farming. The limitless grasslands extending as far as the eye could see meant food for the buffalo, which roamed the Great Plains in the millions. The star-laden night sky inspired the Pawnees, who became famous for their astronomical drawings and observations. For a few hundred years, the Pawnees lived an enviable, golden existence.

2

Pawnee Tribal Life

Compared to most Plains Indians, the Pawnees' lifestyle was unique. They had two styles of home, the tepee and the earth lodge. The tepee was used for times when the Pawnees were on the hunting trail or warpath, or when they were away from their main camp for long periods of time. A tepee could be quickly and single-handedly dismantled, mounted on a travois—a V-shaped frame made with lodge poles, secured to a horse or large dog—and hauled to the next camp site with little trouble. Tepees were constructed with an outer layer of hides, and were surprisingly large, comfortable, and waterproof. Many modern-day tent designs were inspired by the tepee.

The earth lodge was the more permanent dwelling used by the Pawnees. This type of dwelling was usually round, measuring about forty feet in diameter, with large poles as a frame. The round shape was inspired by the night skies so admired by the Pawnees; they built their homes to mirror the shape of the celestial dome. The round shape was also used because it was an innovative wind-deflector: the wind could not blow directly on any side of the structure, since there were no sides, and the construction was perfectly suited to the plains.

The Pawnee technique of mixing mud, grass, and rocks to fill in the gaps between the poles was imitated by the white settlers who came later and created the now-famous Plains "sod" home.

Each Pawnee village comprised about a dozen earth lodges. Each lodge could comfortably hold as many as eight families, housing a total of around forty people. The average size village had a population of approximately five hundred Pawnees. The Pawnees lived in their earth lodges for four to six months out of the year. In the spring and fall they lived in these dwellings, planted and harvested their crops, and prepared themselves and their belongings for another migration.

Like most other Plains tribes, the Pawnee had rules of etiquette for everyone to follow that helped them to get along. There were quite a number of rules in regard to visiting another lodge or tepee. If the door flap was open, this was a sign that the residents were receptive to visitors. If it was closed, the visitors were to announce their presence and wait to be acknowledged and invited inside.

The warmest place, the place next to the fire, was reserved for visitors. Robes were laid there as a sign of welcome, much the way in which modern-day people place welcome mats at a doorway. When entering the lodge or tepee, women followed the men inside. Everyone walked around the entire lodge by way of the east, as there was a sacred spot in every lodge in the west, in front of a buffalo altar. This sacred spot, called *wi-haru,* was reserved for "the place where the wise words of those who have gone before us are resting." It was also considered a breach of etiquette to pass between two people engaged in conversation, or between another person and the fire. Men sat cross-legged. Women sat on their heels or with their legs out to one side.

No one immediately addressed visitors. There was a pause in which guests were allowed to rest a moment, gather their thoughts, and catch their breath. This was the time for the smoking of the pipe. It was only after the pipe smoking that the business at hand or the reason for the visit was mentioned. If the visitors were unexpected, the nature of their business was not to be asked; the Pawnees were infinitely patient and knew that time would reveal what they needed to know. The order of conversation was determined by one's tribal status.

It was always at the conclusion of any discussion that a woman in the lodge served everyone food; the conversation then turned to lighter matters. If the guests had been expected, they brought their own bowls and eating utensils. It was not considered polite to decline food—one should eat all the food one was served. The end of the evening was marked when the host cleaned his pipe. This was the signal for everyone to leave, and they did so with no further talk.

In addition to the regular lodge, the Pawnees also built a *sweat lodge*, similar to a steam bath. Cleanliness was highly valued by every member of the tribe and they often bathed not once but twice daily, regardless of the weather. The sweat lodge was used for personal cleansing and purification rituals.

The survival of the people was dependent in large part on the hunting prowess of its men. To provide their families with meat and hides, the mainstays of their existence, hunting was taken seriously and was carried out in a prescribed manner.

Each hunter made his own bows and arrows, and other weapons such as flint knives. The hunting of the buffalo was done in the summer and winter, but although much of their hunting was buffalo related, the Pawnees also hunted deer, antelope, and elk. The Pawnee hunters were adept at killing jackrabbit and mountain sheep, and they would set snares in which to catch game birds such as quail.

During the spring and fall hunting seasons, the Pawnees moved frequently and thus lived in dwellings such as tepees that they could easily erect. Shown here is a Pawnee scout and interpreter with his family in a tepee.

Most of the Pawnee culture centered upon the buffalo. For the Pawnee and other Plains tribes, the buffalo was tangible proof that Tirawa cared for them. With the gift of bison, Tirawa provided the people with virtually all their needs.

During the hunting seasons, the location of the Pawnee campsite was determined by the herd's movements; the people traveled where the buffalo did. The holy men helped the people locate the buffalo, as did the various wolf-skin-robed scouts. Medicine bundles often included buffalo parts. The Pawnees burned the plains grasses each spring to induce new growth upon which the buffalo fed. This practice encouraged the herds to migrate to the area.

The successful hunter made a life study of the buffalo's characteristics and learned them well. He knew there were different colors of buffalo—one might have a spotted coat, another, a mouse-colored coat. The older a buffalo was, the tougher his flesh and the rougher his fur would be. Thus, if a bison lived to an old age, he was usually safe from the lance and arrow.

The buffalo were not hunted in July, their mating season. This was a dangerous time for anyone to get near a bull bison, which could be quite aggressive. The young buffalo, called a calf, was born in the spring with a birth weight of up to forty pounds. The calf's hair was tinged red or yellow; this was replaced by a darker color by the time the calf was a year old. Many Pawnee children wore robes made with the skin of a newborn calf.

By the next fall, the yearling had developed thick, dark, fluffy fur, and his weight had increased to approximately four hundred pounds. A two-year-old calf began to show the beginnings of horns and had two teeth. The most favored hides came from four-year-old calves, whose fur was silky and thick.

The Pawnees were very imaginative in using all of the buffalo parts they could; there was very little wasted. Each part had many uses. For example, the skin was tanned for winter robes, headdresses, saddle padding, and ornaments. Horns and bones were used for various types of cooking and cultivating implements, and other tools, weapons, and toys. Tendons were dressed and made into especially resilient and strong sinew, which was used for sewing clothing and tepee liners and for making bowstrings. The four-chambered stomach lining was used as a cooking vessel and a type of pail for carrying water. Hooves were used to make ceremonial rattles; dried buffalo dung, or chips were used to fuel fires and to make an effective mosquito repellent when rubbed on clothing and skin. Bison tail hair was braided and made into rope.

Every edible part of the bison was consumed. The tongue and hump were considered delicacies; the liver and heart were often eaten raw, immediately after the kill. Tougher parts of the buffalo were made into *pemmican,* a nutritious blend of pulverized berries mixed with buffalo meat and tallow.

This 1873 photo by William Henry Jackson shows a Pawnee family standing outside their earth lodge. Most Pawnee villages were made up of at least a dozen earth lodges, which could each house up to eight families.

The sheer number of buffalo was in itself enough to inspire an almost spiritual awe in the Pawnees. So great were the numbers of buffalo that it would take hours for a single great herd to cross a stream. It was only natural for the Pawnees to base much of their religion upon this great animal. Medicine men used buffalo skulls in performing their ceremonies; a skull was also placed in front of the entrance to the sweat lodge, facing east, the direction of the rising sun.

Every home had a sacred place reminding the inhabitants of the importance of the buffalo to their lives. Each earth lodge had a raised platform, a kind of altar, on the west wall opposite the entryway. This held a buffalo skull; the lodge's sacred medicine bundle and two ears of corn were suspended above it.

The Pawnees supplemented their diet with fish from the surrounding rivers. Fish were caught with a flint-headed spear or a kind of seine made of willow, reeds, or woven strips of hide. Fish of all types inhabited the big rivers, including a variety of trout, perch, and crappie. Turtles provided a tasty respite from the daily diet.

Pawnee women gathered a great variety of vegetation, taking it as another gift from Tirawa. They foraged for wild peas and more than a dozen different types of wild fruit, including persimmons and chokecherries. Prairie turnips (called *pommes blanches* by the French and Indian Turnips by white settlers) have been said to be the most widely used wild food source. They ripened in the spring to the size of an egg, and were either eaten raw, cooked in soups, or sliced and sun-dried for later use.

Women also gathered and peeled the sweet thistle plant, which tasted similar to a banana. Milkweed buds, rose hips, and the fruit of the prickly pear cactus were flavorful and nutritious; they were often added to buffalo stews.

Seminomadic as they were, the Pawnees nonetheless stayed long enough in one place to cultivate some crops. They planted corn, squash, pumpkins, melons, and beans. The always-practical Pawnee women came up with a clever way to support the bean plants without having to make poles for their gardens. They simply planted the beans at the bases of cornstalks. As the corn grew taller, the beans had a natural pole on which to climb.

Farming was relegated to the Pawnee women, and although every important event in a Pawnee's life called for a ceremony to ask the blessings of Tirawa, the only Pawnee ceremony in which women played a major role was the one in which the spring crops were planted. This was known as the Ground-Breaking Ceremony. During the wintertime, a woman in the village, specially chosen by Tirawa, would have a vision of the ceremony. She told the priests of the village about her vision. The priests would declare her the "visionary" who would be the sponsor of the Ground-Breaking Ceremony. The visionary's brother or nearest living male relative then killed a buffalo especially for her. She dressed the buffalo, prepared the meat, and then stored it in a *cache*, an underground food-storage pit that preserved the meat through the winter.

The tribe's holy men waited for two signs that would show the people it was time for the Ground-Breaking Ceremony to begin. First, the willows along the river had to bud. Then the moon had to hide herself—what we call the dark of the moon—which the Pawnees saw as the time most favorable for germination. The priests then told the visionary it was time to begin. The visionary arose early the next morning, took a special medicine bundle from its hanging place inside the lodge, and hung it outside on a tripod. She then cleaned the lodge and decorated it with willow sprouts.

The four priests then had the woman bring the meat she had prepared for the ceremony, and they also invited four specially chosen women to participate by donating more dried buffalo meat and corn. The group, with a number of other persons of importance, gathered in the ceremonial lodge. The visionary did her special dance for the occasion, and the others shook gourd rattles and sang. Then everyone ate the food that had been brought and stayed up talking and telling stories until the early morning hours.

The next day the Ground-Breaking Ceremony itself took place. The entire ceremony lasted from dawn until sunset. Its major feature was a dance depicting the hoeing of the corn, which was always the first crop to be planted. Then the holy men, using four sacred hoes, ritually broke the ground. After the Ground-Breaking Ceremony, the actual planting began. The people worked at a fever pitch; it took about six days for the entire garden to be weeded, cultivated, and planted. While planting, the Pawnee women sang special songs to "help" the seeds sprout. One way in which Pawnee women helped each other was for a group of women to plant and harvest a newly married bride's first crop.

The environment in which the Pawnees lived provided everything they required to clothe, feed, and shelter themselves. These Pawnee warriors are wearing both traditional clothing, including buffalo robes and bear necklaces, along with blankets supplied by the U.S. government.

Tobacco was another crop of importance to the Pawnees. The ground for the tobacco field was burned bare of all other vegetation. After the tobacco seeds were planted, the field was carefully weeded. When the crop was ripe, the entire tobacco plant was cut and dried. The part of the tobacco plant with the best flavor for smoking was said to be the unripe seed capsules.

The plains provided virtually all that the Pawnee people required for food, shelter, clothing, defense, hunting, and artistic expression. Their workshop was the natural world; they took items from the earth, always giving thanks, as these were gifts from Tirawa. They wasted nothing; to do so would have been a sign of ingratitude. Their tools were made of woods, grasses, stones, bones, plants, clays, and the skins and feathers of various animals.

Pawnee women wove reeds and other natural fibers into mats for their lodge floors and bedding materials. Natural fiber wraps were also used to encase the deceased. These natural fibers were also woven into carrying baskets and small gaming implements, such as gambling trays. A stiff type of grass, called porcupine grass, was made into a kind of hairbrush.

Wood was often made into bowls and mortars, pipe stems, and ceremonial objects. Spoons with beaded handles were made from wood as well as stone. Wood from the elm, chokecherry, dogwood, birch, and willow (among others) went into the making of arrow shafts and bows. Because it was strong yet light, cottonwood was used in tepee and earth lodge construction. The Pawnees were more adept at carpentry than many other Plains tribes. They showed their talents particularly in the making of post-and-beam fittings for their earth lodge frames.

In the making of bull (or basket) boats, the people were once again practical and ingenious in adapting to their environment. The shallow Platte River was virtually unnavigable by the average vessel. But the Pawnees' bull boat was light, with little draft, and was the vessel of choice when the Pawnees plied the waters of the wide Platte.

Stones were sculpted for use as pipe bowls, spoons, and other hollowware for eating and cooking. Buffalo horns were polished, hollowed, and used as quivers for holding arrows. At first, flint and other types of hard stones and bones were made into arrowheads; later, trade with other peoples brought metal that could be used for arrowheads.

There were basically two types of arrowhead—one used in hunting and one used for war. The hunting arrowhead was long, barbless, and tapering. It was firmly attached to the shaft of the arrow. In this way, after the kill, the entire weapon could be easily removed, saving it for another hunt.

The war arrowhead was made to function in just the

opposite manner. It was heavier than a hunting arrowhead, and its head was barbed to make extraction nearly impossible (not to mention excruciating for the wounded enemy). The war arrowhead was attached to the shaft in such a way that, with any effort made to remove it from a wound, the shaft and head would separate. If this happened the wounded enemy-warrior would almost certainly suffer a painful and drawn-out death.

Arrow shafts were painted to identify their owner. This was particularly useful in a large hunting group, such as accompanied the semiannual buffalo hunt; everyone knew in this way which animals were their responsibility to butcher.

In processing killed animals, stones and bones played extremely useful roles. Both were used in the cutting of flesh, in the making of tools from various animal parts, and in the sewing of animal hides to make clothes and tepee covers. Sharp, broad stones were also used in food preparation, especially in the making of pemmican. Many larger bones were used in agriculture. The broad, strong shoulder blade of the buffalo, for example, was used as a spade or a hoe.

Most of the plants important to the Pawnees were of the edible variety. But in addition to weaving grasses for mats, the Pawnees used various plants in the dyeing and decorating of their clothes, tepees, or possessions, such as a pipe stem or a war pony's hide. Many hide blankets were dyed black with water boiled with sumac leaves.

The pigments in various types of earth were used in painting, as well as in the dyeing of hides. To dye a hide blanket white, for example, a fine white clay was rubbed into the hide after tanning, then allowed to dry before being removed.

Clay was used primarily in the making of pottery, a talent for which the Pawnees are especially noted. The making of clay into pottery required many steps. First, a mold was made from a smoothed-out tree trunk. Then stones were "roasted" for a long time in a hot fire, ground, and made into a fine powder. This powder was mixed with clay, then smeared over the mold which was well greased with buffalo fat. While the clay was still pliable, the Pawnees made sharp marks in the sides for ornamentation, then lifted it from the mold. The clay form was then burned in the fire. While it was baking, the Pawnees put corn in the pot and stirred it, making a kind of natural glaze on the inside of the pot.

The resulting pottery was extremely hard and durable enough to hang over a cooking fire. Pottery excavated from Pawnee villages has a shape characteristic of the Pawnee method of pottery making, with a large, globular bottom and a thick rim. This rim was used by the cook, who secured a rawhide "handle" around it, to carry it or hang it from the cooking fire.

The skins of animals were also important to Pawnee daily life and survival. Tepee covers, moccasins, saddles, ropes and whips, *parfleches* (a bag made from animal skin), and a kind of water bucket all came from various types of hide. Hides also were used for making skin shirts, which were worn by men of high standing.

There were basically three stages of skin, or hide, preparation. The first stage produced rawhide, in which the hair was removed from the skin. The second stage—tanning—produced a hide that was softer and more pliable than rawhide. To tan, the hide was stretched on a kind of frame, and a mixture of elm bark and buffalo brains was worked into the hide. Skins could be tanned with or without hair.

The third step in hide preparation was dyeing. Hides were often dyed a light yellow color by smoking them over a fire made with rotten wood. Clothing was usually dyed this color; the skins most often used for clothing were deer and elk, as they were the softest.

Feathers were used on headdresses, fans, lances, war clubs, coup sticks, shields, hair decorations, and pipe stems. In feathering or fletching arrow shafts, the feathers were placed in such a way as to provide a spin to the loosed arrow, giving it a motion similar to that of a bullet fired from a rifle. This made the trajectory of the arrow more stable and accurate. Feathers were usually obtained from the eagle, wild turkey, hawk, and owl.

Preparation for the actual hunt was a protracted process involving travel, ceremony, and discipline. Once the traveling band got near a herd, the entire camp of men, women, and children were under a certain amount of restraint. This restraint was ensured by a special society, the *Hunt Police*. The night before the big hunt, a group of men were appointed for this job. The police would then patrol the camp to make certain that all was quiet and that no hunter had gone out alone. If this happened, even though he might get one buffalo, the entire herd could be stampeded and the tribe could lose its chance at getting enough meat for everyone.

The dog that barked unnecessarily that night might be killed on the spot. Children were not allowed to cry or play any noisy games. The people were not even allowed to chop wood.

Hours before dawn, several scouts were assigned to a reconnaissance mission. Getting very close to the herd, the scouts would crawl on their bellies, imitating the wolf, of which the bison were not afraid. Sometimes the scouts would even wear wolf skins.

Returning to the camp, the scouts would tell of the number and location of the herd; the chiefs would devise a plan from this information. The women broke camp quickly, taking care to free up as many horses as possible for the hunt. As the people continued these preparations, the medicine man, or *shaman*, would dance in the impersonation of a buffalo and sing a chant that went something like this:

> Now you are going to trot
> Buffalo who are killed falling.

He would then fall down as if dead for anyone in the camp who would give him tobacco.

One of the chiefs made a member of the hunting party the official starter, or "hand waver." As they rode closer to the herd, one of the scouts would signal how fast to come and in what direction, depending on what he thought the buffalo herd was about to do. Sometimes the hand waver would hesitate, inadvertently testing the hunters' patience. He waited until he felt his own personal medicine was as good as it was going to get. Any hunter starting before the signal would often get a severe clubbing by the Hunt Police; order was, therefore, usually not difficult to maintain.

At the signal, the hunters sped toward the herd, sometimes shouting to each other the equivalent of "That one's going to be mine!" Any good Pawnee hunter could fire arrows almost as fast as a rifleman could shoot, and they sometimes did it with such force that an arrow would go completely through a buffalo, even as it ran at full speed.

The Pawnee custom was to have two main meals each day. Although most of the food preparation was done by women, the chores were divided so that no one did more than her fair share. In the earth lodge, the women on the south side prepared one meal, the women on the north the other. Each side fed all the occupants of the earth lodge, or about fifty persons. Willing hands were never lacking, as it was an honor to volunteer to work in any capacity that would benefit everyone. Laziness or the shirking of one's duties was unheard of.

The mainstay of each meal was first buffalo and then corn. Corn was prepared in many ways. It was boiled, dried, roasted, made into a mush, added to soup or stew, or pounded to a powder and used as flour. The pottery mentioned earlier was the type of cooking vessel most commonly used by the Pawnees, although there are some accounts of their making stews and soups using the stomach lining from a buffalo. Since this type of cooking vessel was not fireproof, however, the stew was cooked by dropping in large stones that were first heated in a fire. The hot stones were stirred around in the food mixture, cooking the stew quickly.

Drying foodstuffs, especially meats, was an ingenious method of food preservation devised by the Pawnee and other food-gathering tribes. Pawnee women stored preserved food in a cache, which kept foods cool and dry and delayed the process of decay. The pit was usually about eleven feet deep and bell-shaped, with smooth walls. The floor was covered with sand and then bark. American explorers such as Meriwether Lewis and William Clark were quick to take note of this ingenious method of food storage and preservation; they employed it in their travels, digging caches in places to which they intended to return.

When a woman cooked a meal, she did virtually every step in its preparation herself. The vegetables and fruits had been raised and gathered by her own hands. She had butchered and dried the meat she served; the bread came from a grain that she herself grew and made into flour. She had most likely dug the cache and made the cooking implements, such as the pottery, the wooden bowls and spoons, and even the grass mats upon which everyone sat.

Women's everyday clothing consisted of a buckskin dress or wraparound skirt with an overblouse and leggings. If the weather was fair, children of both sexes often wore nothing when they were very young. Later, a girl's clothing was a smaller version of what her mother wore. For special occasions, the leggings were beaded and painted.

Men's and boys' clothing usually consisted of a *breechclout* (a type of loincloth), a buckskin shirt, and leggings. The shirt was usually worn loose. The Pawnee man wore not one but two belts. The first belt held up his breechclout and leggings. The second was made from thick hide and on this belt he hung his tomahawk, knife, and gun, as well as his pipe, tobacco pouch, and whetstone.

During the winter, Pawnee men and women often wore buffalo robes, with the fur-side turned in and the skin side turned out so that they could display designs such as this group of stars.

Every man had a buffalo robe that he kept close at hand in his lodge. He threw it over his shoulders or around his waist to receive visitors. Those in high standing wore special clothing. The skin shirt was for those in the very highest of ranks and regard. This shirt was decorated with scalps lining the sleeves, and porcupine quillwork running the length of the shirtfront. A man who had done exceptionally well in battle wore an otter skin around his neck. Many warriors wore turbans of different colors and designs to denote their rank.

Moccasins were left plain for everyday use but were decorated for special occasions. Burial moccasins were usually beaded and painted. Festival moccasins and wedding moccasins were beaded and decorated with elaborate quillwork. The Pawnee, like many other tribes of the Great Plains, had their own uniquely shaped and decorated style of moccasin. Following the trail of the enemy was thus made easier; however, sometimes a warrior would steal moccasins from a fallen enemy and wear those to throw off any would-be pursuers.

So closely did the Pawnee people relate to the astronomical bodies—everything the People did was in relationship to the celestial bodies and the earth—that they considered their earth lodges to be smaller versions of the universe. The lodge was built in such a way that, through the smoke hole at the top, the western stars could be observed, and the eastern skies could be viewed through the door flap. Just before dawn and right after sunset, the people would observe the horizon, taking note of the position and courses of the stars.

The performance of rituals and chores, such as the *Morning Star Ceremony* and the planting of the garden, centered upon these cosmic observations. When on the hunt, the way in which the Pawnees grouped their tepees followed an astronomical pattern, mimicking what they saw in the sky. The Pawnees had an acute sense of the position and order of the stars, and they are noted for their artistic interpretations of the skies. For example, rawhide containers in which they packed dried buffalo meat were painted with cosmic designs. Different patterns and colors were used for the moon, stars, and even the time of night. The artist who painted these designs had to be specially trained and had to possess the proper spiritual qualifications.

One type of Pawnee war bonnet was fashioned after a comet. The bonnet was decorated with eagle feathers, long strings of white beads (symbolizing the comet's "tail"), and a large shiny disk made with a black oyster shell.

Knowledge of the constellations also had a more practical use. A person could easily become disoriented on the vast plains, much in the same way that a sailor at sea might lose his way without knowledge of the stars. The earliest explorers were amazed at how adept the Pawnees were in traveling across the plains and at how they always knew their precise location.

The chief of the tribe held his power through divine ordinance because his wisdom was a gift from Tirawa. He was also in possession of the tribe's sacred bundle, given to the Pawnees by First Man. However, there was no one chief who ruled over all four Pawnee bands; rather, each village had its own chief. The chief was no great wielder of power. His position was more like the head of a very large family, a sort of administrative official. This was a natural outcome of the Pawnee way of voluntarism and independence, and it suited their lifestyle well.

There were occasions when the son of a chief also attained chiefdom, but a spirit of humility, calm wisdom, and cooperation played a more important role in the people's choice. When a chief took note of a promising young man with ambitions to become a chief, the older man would take the younger man into his lodge to serve a kind of apprenticeship.

The Pawnee community also had shamans, or medicine men. The term "medicine man" is a word first employed by European explorers, who witnessed shamanistic activities without understanding them. In Pawnee culture there existed what have been called "doctor cults." These were organizations of men who practiced varying kinds and degrees of medicine and were more akin to clubs than cults.

The Pawnees believed there were two separate realms, one of the sky and one of the earth and water. The holy man was consulted about all things having to do with the sky, such as cosmic ceremonies. These included the Morning Star, harvesting, planting, and creation ceremonies. The shaman was concerned with the animals, including humankind, who were part of the earth and water.

The shamans believed that long ago Tirawa had entered a man's dreams, teaching him the wisdom of the animals. The man learned about the healing power of special herbs, roots, and songs. That is how shamanism came to the people. When someone, in a dream or vision, received a sign that he too should become a shaman, he would apprentice himself to one. As an apprentice, he sometimes shared the lodge, ran errands, and cooked and served meals when the shamans were in council.

After his apprenticeship, the new shaman was elected into one of eight "doctor cults." Each cult held at least two ceremonies a year, as well as "mesmerizing contests," as any good shaman was also skilled in hypnotism. The cults occasionally gathered together into one large-scale "Doctor Lodge." If a person was found to be conducting medical or ceremonial practices and was not a member of a cult, that person was considered a witch and treated with contempt.

Although it appears that the Pawnee lodge was matriarchal in nature, many of the tasks of men and women were shared. Men as well as women were able cooks and adept at tasks such as sewing and child care. Pawnee women were generally held in high esteem. In preparing and providing food, clothing, and shelter for her family, in the bearing and rearing of children, and in her duties of moving the camp, the Pawnee woman did her chores with dignity and a sense of pride and fulfillment.

With the rough life into which children were born, infant mortality was relatively high. Children were therefore highly regarded. Children ensured continuity for the people; they were possessors of the future. With the stars being so much a part of Pawnee life, everyone, even children, was thought to be born under the guardianship of a given star, thereby making everyone in the tribal village cosmically related. Furthermore, each person's cosmic guardian delineated what that person would or could become, such as a chief, shaman, or brave. Boys had more of a social life than girls. In general, children were allowed to play only with those children whose parents held similar rank.

Men could make themselves near-legendary figures in the eyes of the people by their valor in battle or on the hunt. Warriors most often brought honor to themselves by *counting coup*, touching an enemy without killing him, which took unusual courage if he were armed. Warriors carried "coup

Witchcraft and the Pawnees

Pawnee beliefs have historically included that of witchcraft, and among the Pawnees there are still tribal members who believe that people can be "witched," or have a spell cast on them. In Pawnee beliefs, men or women can be or become witches.

One story from the Skidi Pawnee band tells of how this came to be. Long ago, their people observed animals and saw how they made magic. When those people learned how to perform the rituals surrounding the magic, they could transform themselves into animals. Like the European belief of a witch's "familiar," the animal of choice for the Pawnees was the owl.

Another story, also from the Skidi Pawnee, tells of a man who learned to change into a turkey. In this shape, he would visit the grave of a recently deceased tribal member, exhume the body, remove body parts and either eat them or use them to make more spells. When the rest of the people discovered what the "turkey-witch" was doing, they killed him.

Similar legends concern those of doctors who could not only use their healing powers for good, but learned to cause illness, as well as heal people through the use of magic. There are stories from long ago that tell of someone paying a doctor to put a spell on someone else, to make them ill or die. Usually this was done out of envy, revenge, or hatred. When Christianity was introduced to the Pawnee people, many embraced it as a way of preventing themselves from becoming "witched" or "hexed."

INDIAN RECORD
of a
BATTLE
between the PAWNEES
and the
KONZAS.

A FAC SIMILE
of a
Delineation
upon a
BISON ROBE.

Pawnee men recorded many events on buffalo robes and tepee covers, including buffalo hunts and battles. Shown here is a depiction of a battle between the Pawnee and Konza, or Kansa, Indians which dates to the mid-eighteenth century.

sticks" expressly for this purpose. To a lesser degree, the taking of scalps was also considered a form of counting coup, as was the stealing of horses. Often, when warriors successfully fought against the enemy, they would use charcoal or soft stones to draw pictographs where other enemies coming into the area might find them—a kind of rudimentary warning sign against trespassing.

Hunters were important to the tribe because they provided the people with food. Hunters usually dressed plainly, unless they were engaged in a more formally organized buffalo hunt. The more organized hunt usually included more than one band; there might be up to a hundred men participating. For this type of buffalo hunt, the men dressed in specially decorated leggings and moccasins; those of exceptional rank or prowess wore a skin shirt or tied a bright red bandanna around their heads. The hunting horses were painted in the same manner as their masters. Hunt Police carried clubs and wore belts to symbolize their office.

Warriors and hunters took part in ceremonies and rituals before a battle, raid, or hunt. Warriors also played a major role in harvesttime ceremonies. The dress of warriors in actual battle was as little as the weather would permit, usually little more than moccasins and a breechclout. The ever-practical Pawnees understood that clothing entering the skin along with a bullet or arrow was what caused the most pain and subsequent infection.

As with other aspects of Pawnee life, the activity of going to battle was accompanied by song. One song warriors sang as they rode along goes like this:

> Let us see, is this real,
> This life I am living?
> Ye Gods who dwell everywhere,
> Let us see, is this real,
> This life I am living?

Perhaps the song expressed a fear of dying and the transitory nature of life. Even strong warriors sought to make sense of the constant struggle to survive, long before the name of any god other than Tirawa was spoken in their realm.

Pawnee society also featured a number of specialized societies, clubs, or clans. Hunters, warriors, or even women of vision could be in specialized societies, which held ceremonies and dances when the stars were auspicious. The cults, or clubs, had such names as Black-tailed Deer, Eagle, Reindeer, Buffalo, and Coyote. One such club, the Society of Lucky Children, was not made up of children but adults. In their gatherings, they sat on their mats and recounted lucky things that had happened to them, their tribe, or their ancestors.

The Pawnee language derives from its Caddoan ancestry and is a language group shared by the Caddo, Wichita, Arikara, and Pawnee peoples. Of the Pawnees' four bands (Chaui, Pitahawirata, Kitkahahki, and the Skiri, or Skidi), however, the Skidi or "Wolf" band speaks a different dialect from the other three, probably because it is more separate geographically.

The linguistic diversity among tribes created a need for intertribal communication. Some say that it was a need for trade among tribes that led to the development of sign language; but regardless, this intertribal language of the Plains nations is a beautiful and graceful thing to behold. Sign language was practical in that communication could be accomplished even if the communicants were a certain distance apart, which helped if they were uncertain whether they were speaking to friend or foe. Some experts have pointed to a relationship between sign language and Native American pictographs. Many single signs, with a wave of the arms or indication of direction, represented entire phrases or sentences. The "speaker" could also communicate with movements of his horse.

Other ways of signaling over long distances included the use of ropes, blankets, mirrors, or smoke signals. At close range, such as in battle, flags, lances, or hand and arm signals would be employed. Whistles made from the bone of a turkey leg or an eagle's wing were used in such a way as to be heard over the din of battle. With a series of prearranged whistles, the warring party would know whether they should attack or retreat.

One practice unique to the Pawnees, which they clung to even into the nineteenth century, was that of human sacrifice. The Morning Star Ceremony was the second spring ritual conducted by the tribal holy men, the first being the retelling of the creation myth. The Morning Star Ceremony included the sacrifice of a young child, usually a girl, taken from an enemy tribe. The Pawnees believed that this sacrifice was to pay homage to the god of the Morning Star for his efforts during the earth's creation, to guarantee that he would deliver a good crop, and ensure fertility for the women of the tribe. Since the

Many Pawnee ceremonies—both secular and religious—involved the sharing of a ceremonial pipe, which Pawnee men would smoke communally.

Pawnees also believed that the first person on Earth was female, this was also their way of symbolically "returning" her to Morning Star.

According to tribal legend, the ceremony began with a young warrior's vision of the Morning Star speaking to him. The warrior told a tribal priest, and they shared a ceremonial pipe. The warrior next chose a small contingent to go with him to the enemy tribe, to abduct the maiden to be sacrificed.

The priest ceremonially prepared and dressed the warrior in a buffalo-hair rope belt, a collar made of otter skin, a hawk's skin around his neck, and an ear of corn on his left shoulder. The warrior's face was painted with two streaks of red down each cheek and a bird's footprint on his forehead. Dressed in this way, the warrior and his companions departed as the Morning Star rose.

Approaching the enemy camp (some accounts claim that Pawnees usually targeted Sioux), the Pawnee band surrounded them and attacked on a given signal. They were instructed to harm no one unless it was necessary, but to look for a girl of about thirteen who would then be pronounced holy for the Great Star.

The group carried the girl back to camp, where she was treated well until the holy men deemed it was the right time for the ceremony. The girl was then given a smoke bath, which involved passing her over a fire made with sweet-smelling grasses, as a way to purify her. She was painted with a mixture of red pigment and buffalo fat and dressed in fine calfskin, a thick buffalo robe, and soft down moccasins. The girl was also given special eating utensils, to be used only by her.

For several days the unsuspecting maiden was treated with utmost respect and honored with singing and dancing and feasting, even as the sacrificial scaffold was being prepared. Finally, as dawn approached on the appointed day, the procession to the scaffold began. All male members of the tribe were to take part. The visionary warrior, dressed in his ceremonial clothing, tied the girl's wrists with elk-skin rope and led the procession. Four holy men carried sacred bundles, each representing one of the cardinal directions. On the way to the scaffold, the people sang four songs for the animals the Evening Star had placed in the semi-cardinal directions—the bear, the mountain lion, the wildcat, and the wolf.

The girl was led atop the scaffold and bound by her wrists, standing upright, facing the direction of the sunrise. Without warning, just as the sun rose, one of the holy men completed the sacrifice by shooting the maiden through the heart with his bow and arrow. Some of her blood was used to anoint a specially consecrated buffalo heart and tongue, which were then ceremonially burned. Afterward, each male of the tribe, even the little babies, who of course needed help, shot an arrow into the maiden's body. After this, she was taken down and returned to earth to allow her blood to fertilize the ground. The Morning Star Ceremony was followed by much celebration and what one witness described as "ceremonial sexual licensure."

The ages considered most auspicious for marriage were fifteen for girls and eighteen for boys, but with first marriages for both sexes there was often as much as a fifteen-year age difference between husband and wife. The reason for this was that a mature man was expected to care not only for his new wife but for her entire family as well. After marriage, the husband usually lived with his wife's family; the family thus looked upon suitors in terms of their ability to become providers for the family group.

Young boys were often married to older women who were not in as much need of a provider as were their younger counterparts. When they matured into grown men, they would then choose a younger bride. In this way, the needs of the mature and the needs of the young who were unable to provide for themselves were all met. Though the idea of polygyny may be offensive to modern sensibilities, it worked out well for the Pawnees at the height of their civilization.

Permission for marriage was sought with the giving of gifts. If she were quite young and unmarried, her suitor might bring as many as half a dozen horses to her father's herd. The bride-price of a mature woman might be one or two horses; these were given to her nearest male relative, such as a brother.

With such fluid relationships, the Pawnees were not without some rules. The paternity of children had to be absolutely certain. Toward this end, a woman was "faithful" to one man for one month at a time. When she discovered her pregnancy, she would thus be able to point out his obligations to the soon-to-be-father. The father was expected to provide for his off-spring, regardless of whose lodge they resided in. If any woman broke this rule of "serial monogamy," it would be the resulting offspring who would suffer. Children without clear paternity were regarded as outcasts by the entire tribe.

A lodge's occupants changed each time the people returned from the buffalo hunt. A family that had been in one lodge for a season might desire to lodge with a different group the next season. This allowed the Pawnees to cultivate an even greater spirit of interdependence and cooperation.

Families lived in ways that would teach the young a spirit of cooperation and provide both young and old with constant companionship and a sense of security. The idea of a nursing home, for example, is completely alien to traditional Pawnee philosophy.

Certain aspects of Pawnee home life seem to have been matriarchal in nature. As mentioned earlier, the food preparation chores of the earth lodge were equally divided by women in the north and south sectors of the lodge. Other chores were divided mostly according to age. Places the women assumed within the lodge itself were also determined by age.

The mature women occupied the central portion of the lodge's north and south sectors; their chores were to provide the main provisions and direct the efforts of the other, younger women. In the western sectors of these two halves, the young girls and newlywed women resided; the eastern sectors were taken by the elderly women. They were placed here because, symbolically, they were on their way out of life, and were thus placed near the door.

The able hunter was the nucleus of each lodge, but men in general could sleep anywhere they chose. Young men might stay in any lodge on any given night; for them, sleeping mats were placed between the central pillars of the lodge. Old men were also free to stay wherever they pleased, usually becoming an overnight guest of the lodge in which they fell asleep telling stories to the occupants.

The married man's household, that of his wife, was not considered his real home. He lived in his wife's lodge because of his obligations to their marriage and to her family. Sometimes his duties might overwhelm him; then he would leave for a few days and stay at the home of his sisters or mother. This was always considered his real home, and the wife was expected to understand.

There were other men who never had any real responsibilities within the tribe. These men the people called boys regardless of their age. The boys roamed about freely and gave away their possessions even as they obtained them. Sometimes they were recognized as braves for their service to the people.

During pregnancy, many women of the Plains tribes practiced walking in the early morning hours because they believed that this was the time of day the baby grew. Before the baby's birth, the mother or grandmother would make special "medicine" for the child, in the form of two beaded and quilled amulets. One was in the form of a lizard, which they believed frightened away malevolent forces; the other was a turtle, known for its longevity and for being difficult to kill. These amulets would be particularly useful if the infant was a boy.

When it came time for the child to be born, a woman in labor usually went to her home lodge. If the tribe was on the move, she had to give birth out in the open, alongside the trail. Older women attended the birth. The physician or shaman might also attend, singing songs to ensure an easy delivery and a healthy infant. If things got difficult, the priest would come and decorate the turtle amulet with a tortoise charm, to shield the baby from any dangers in the birthing process.

After birth, the umbilical cord was severed, wrapped in herbs or tobacco, and packed inside the turtle amulet. This amulet was later worn on the child's clothing as a reminder of the gift of life it had received from its parents. If a warrior attained greatness, he might wear this amulet on his headdress. Several days after birth, the baby was given a name, usually by the father. This name might be changed later if the child, especially a boy child, achieved high status within the tribe or had a life-changing experience.

When an elderly Pawnee felt that he or she had had enough of life, that person would simply walk away from the village and never return. But when people fell ill and died, or were killed in battle or in the hunt, they were given a burial whenever possible. The deceased were dressed in their best clothes, and specially beaded burial moccasins were placed on their feet. The deceased was often wrapped in a blanket or a covering made of reeds, grasses, or hide. The body was laid to rest in a high place, to be nearer the Creator, usually in a burial scaffold or tree. The family would also hang some of the deceased's favorite possessions nearby. If the dead person had been a great warrior, his favorite horse would sometimes be killed to accompany him to the other side, although this might be protested by family members hoping to inherit the animal. A grieving widow often cut off her hair and at least one of her fingers.

Among Native American peoples, grave robbing was unheard of; places of burial were considered inviolable. Even if a weaponless, hungry warrior, lost from his tribe, came upon a burial site in which there were plenty of knives, guns, and other provisions, he would not desecrate the site by stealing.

Babies and children in Pawnee society were considered gifts from Tirawa and thus were treated with a great deal of indulgence that was sometimes frowned upon by early white explorers. Because their lives were centered in a group of intermingled personalities from their earliest days, Pawnee children learned from and were cared for by a myriad of persons in the tribe.

In Pawnee society, babies were thought to be gifts who were presented to the family by the Pawnee god, Tirawa. However, the burden of raising the child did not fall solely to the parents; rather it was the responsibility of the entire village to help nurture the child.

Formal discipline was not really needed for Pawnee children. The greatest disciplinarian was the children's environment. Pawnee children were taught from their first breath that strict self-control and cooperation were intrinsic to their survival. Every day they were shown harsh examples of what would happen if they were to do otherwise.

A hunter going out alone, in defiance of the Hunt Police, might be ambushed and killed by a marauding enemy band. He might stampede the buffalo herd upon which the tribe depended, which could result in a food shortage. Children learned by example to be honorable, courageous, industrious, and generous, and grew to dread anything that would bring them the contempt or criticism of their peers.

Right after a child was weaned, he or she was given over to the "grandmother," who was often an unrelated elderly woman. She was then the major provider for the child's care. The child shared the same bed and even the same meal bowl with the grandmother.

At play, children mimicked their elders. Girls played with miniature tepees and tiny dolls in cradle boards made with sticks. Boys played games in which they pretended to "count coup," or kill buffalo. But when boys and girls reached the age of adolescence, they were no longer allowed to play together.

When a Pawnee boy reached the age of about ten, the mother often sent him to her brother's lodge. The uncle then taught the boy all he would need to know for survival and life. This instruction went as far as the sharing of the uncle's wife (or wives) with the nephew. When the boy was about twelve, he went on his first hunt with his fellow tribesmen. Later, he would accompany his father and perhaps an uncle or two on a raid of an enemy camp. Pawnees knew that early praise was an invaluable teaching tool and gave it as often as possible.

Girls were taught at an early age to think of their future responsibilities. They were encouraged to have their own beds as early as possible and not to be coddled. Girls were raised to expect that one day they would care for their brothers much as their mother did. Even once established in lodges of their own, their home was always considered their brothers' "real" home, regardless of whom each married. The fathers would some-times tell the sons, "Be nice to your sister; one day she'll be tak-ing care of you."

As the girl grew into womanhood, she learned and became proficient in all the important things a Pawnee woman needed to know. She learned to sew moccasins, fashion beadwork, cook, and dress and tan buffalo hides and other game. By the time she was of marriageable age, she could dismantle a tepee, load a travois, and be on the move in less than half an hour. She was advised by the older women how to receive suitors and care for the family she would one day have. The Pawnee female was raised to take pride in herself as a woman and in all her accomplishments. A woman who was thrifty, talented, and industrious earned the respect and admiration of all the people.

Pawnee society as a whole was rather fluid, with no firmly established mores or punishments forcibly imposed on the people. When someone committed a socially repugnant act, he or she was treated as a social outcast. Outcasts were typically children with no clear paternity or people accused of witchcraft. But there was another type of outcast: the person who had been scalped, who could never return to the tribe. They lived on the fringes of the populace and were regarded with fear. The scalped person, even though he or she had survived such an ordeal, was forced to live alone, in a dugout in an embankment, stealing whatever they needed to survive.

3

The Pawnee World Changes Forever

For centuries, the Pawnees lived a challenging but golden existence in relative peace. Then the season of change was upon them.

The first non-Native American people to meet the Pawnees were the members of a Spanish expedition headed by Francisco Vásquez de Coronado. It was the middle of the sixteenth century and the world was witnessing international upheaval. Henry VIII of England declared himself king of Ireland, and married and then beheaded his fifth wife, Catherine Howard. In Japan, Portuguese explorers landed, bringing firearms to Asia. The Vatican intensified its campaign to root out heresy through the Inquisition. Many countries were seeking to expand their landholdings, including Spain.

The 29-year-old Coronado was dispatched to "New Spain," as the American territories were called, with 300 Spanish conquistadors, 800 Indian allies, five Franciscan priests, and a few black slaves. Coronado's ambition was to explore New Spain's northernmost boundaries and to move beyond them into the wilderness. The Spanish crown believed that located in this area were several cities of such wealth that they were made of gold. Coronado himself believed this to the extent that he provided nearly half the funds for the expedition—roughly $2 million in today's currency.

Coronado and his men traveled across Texas, Oklahoma, and on into the territory of Kansas. A slave had assured them that there was indeed a golden city there, called *Quivira*. Once in this region, Coronado and his men were rewarded not with gold but with winds gusting up to eighty miles an hour, shadeless plains with wildly erratic weather, and huge herds of buffalo resembling great dark clouds as they thundered across the plains. This was about as far north as Coronado would travel in his search for the fabled Seven Cities of Gold. He had been on the trail of Quivira for more than a year by the time his soldiers first saw the Pawnees.

A reconnaissance group sent farther north came upon a large group of Pawnees encamped on the present-day Republican River. The Pawnees were probably astonished to see men wearing metal armor and helmets, with hairy faces (Pawnee men plucked all their facial hair), sitting astride great four-footed beasts that did the work of camp dogs but were large enough to be ridden.

The Pawnees were quick to obtain these wonderful new animals for themselves, using various means to do so. The Pawnees and other Plains tribes came to know that wherever explorers, hunters, and trappers were, horses would be found. They went on increasingly daring raids for horses and whatever other plunder they could take.

The coming of the horse to Pawnee life and culture enlarged their hunting area, made traveling easier and faster, and helped make warriors more effective in battle. The horse also made the Pawnee women's work easier. Instead of loading a travois onto the back of a working dog, a woman could now load not only tepee implements but other things that she might otherwise have carried herself. Children, who before had to be carried, rode on horseback or atop a travois. The number of horses one owned became a status symbol; the giving of horses in settling a dispute or as a bride-price became part of Pawnee culture.

Among the Pawnee people today there is a horse that carries special "medicine": the dun pony. Dun horses have a grayish-yellow coat and black mane and tail, and there is an ancient legend surrounding the dun pony that goes something like this: Long ago, there was a boy everyone called Dirty Belly. He lived alone with his grandmother, and for reasons unclear, they were outcasts from the rest of the tribe. They were not allowed to go with everyone else on the buffalo hunt, and could only gather what was left over from the hunting-field after everyone else had butchered and taken what they wanted. They lived apart from everyone else, and everyone made fun of Dirty Belly, because they said he would never amount to anything—he did not even have a horse of his own.

One afternoon, as he and his grandmother were gleaning the hunting-field for leftover meat, Dirty Belly spied an abandoned dun pony. He had been wounded, was dirty and swaybacked. "No one wanted him," the grandmother told Dirty Belly. "If we were Apache, we could eat him, but we do not eat horses; let us leave him for the coyotes." Dirty Belly refused to leave the dun pony to die, and took him to their lodge to care for him.

The dun pony grew strong and healthy again under Dirty Belly's care. One day the chief sent out the young braves on a hunt to go catch a special buffalo. He wanted its mottled coat for his own lodge, and promised his daughter in marriage and some horses in exchange for this gift. Dirty Belly rode out with the dun pony, despite his entire tribe making fun of him for trying to hunt the buffalo. When Dirty Belly returned, bearing the mottled coat from the buffalo he had killed, he refused the chief's daughter's hand and gave the coat to his grandmother.

The dun pony's medicine helped Dirty Belly get more horses for his lodge, and gave him special medicine in battle. The legend says that as long as Dirty Belly listened to the dun pony and did as he said, there would always be a special bond between such horses and the Pawnee people.

Between Coronado's explorations in 1541 and the beginning of the nineteenth century, the Pawnee people enjoyed a time of prosperity and power—then their land was sold in a deal struck between Napoleon Bonaparte of France and President Thomas Jefferson of the United States. Under the reign of King Louis XVI, France had acquired land in the New World from Spain. In 1803, the new ruler of France, Napoleon, needed money to finance an anticipated war with England. He agreed to sell the land to the Americans. In what has since been called "the greatest diplomatic coup in American history," the United States was able to double its size through this single real estate transaction. For a mere $15 million, the country had obtained an additional 830,000 square miles of territory.

With the Louisiana Purchase, the United States acquired lands extending from the Mississippi River, west to the Rockies, from Texas and Louisiana, north to the Canadian border. But America would have to impose her sovereignty upon the newly acquired territory. Opposition to this came not only from Native Americans but from Great Britain, Russia, and Spain. Spain in fact refused to recognize the validity of the deal and threatened military expeditions to enforce its claim that the borders of New Spain extended north to the Platte River.

Claims to new territories were easier to enforce if those territories were settled, and to settle them it was first necessary to explore and map them. Meriwether Lewis, then a secretary to the president, and William Clark, were appointed to lead an expedition into the newly acquired wilderness. The discoveries of the Lewis and Clark Expedition made them perhaps the most celebrated of American explorers, and helped to establish the idea that it was America's "Manifest Destiny" to extend her boundaries all the way to the Pacific Ocean.

In 1806, another adventurer and explorer, Zebulon Pike, was charged with advising all the Native Americans he encountered that their first loyalties were to the United States and not to Spain, and reminding English traders that they were doing business on American soil. But Spain sent Don Facundo Malgares with an army of six hundred dragoons who impressed the Pawnees, among others. Seeing his force of men and mounted militia, the Pawnees readily accepted Spanish flags and medals, swore allegiance to Spain, and promised to

Lewis and Clark: A Means of Promoting Native People

The summer of 1806 was an eventful one for not only Lewis and Clark's Corps of Discovery but for the Plains Indians as a whole. While the Corps of Discovery had more interaction with other Plains Indian tribes, their visit nonetheless marked the beginning of a season of change that would forever affect the Pawnees.

When the explorers returned to Washington, D.C., with stories of shining mountains; forests teaming with an abundance of game; unbroken, clear streams; and available lands as far as the eye could see, it was too great a temptation for those wanting to make a better life for themselves and their families, and for those wanting to make their fortunes in the West. The end of the Lewis and Clark expedition was the beginning of the great migration, a flood of people that would not stop until the Pawnees were nearly annihilated.

Thus, for more than two centuries, the First Nations regarded any celebration of white exploration—such as Columbus Day—as something to be scorned. Now, in the twenty-first century, however, attitudes are beginning to change. A new attitude has emerged, and now the Pawnee people, along with other tribal nations, have been in support of celebrating the Lewis and Clark

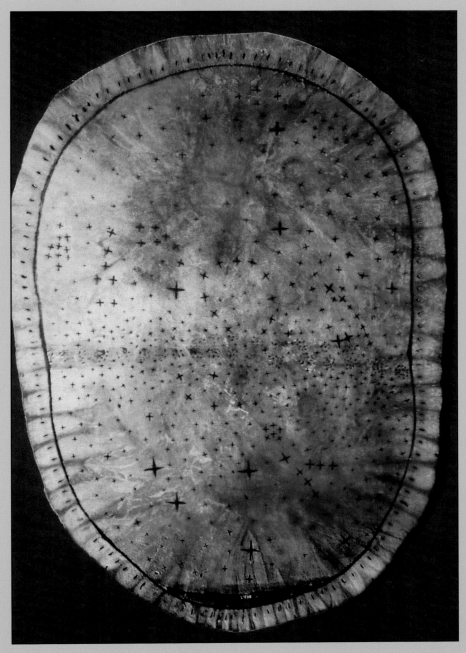

This chart made of buckskin represents the night sky and is housed at the Field Museum of Natural History in Chicago. Many of the Pawnees' ceremonies revolved around the cosmos and they had an acute sense of the position and order of the stars.

This wood cradle board served to support a skin baby-carrier, which the Pawnees used during their travels. The symbol at the top represents the Morning Star, which rises in the East every morning and plays a significant role in Pawnee lore.

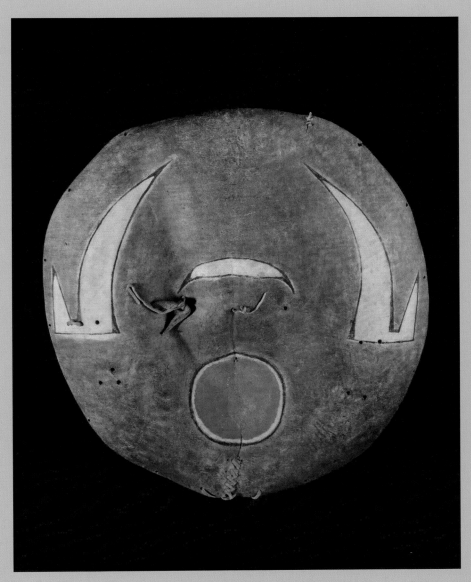

Many Pawnee warriors decorated their shields with astronomical signs, such as the sun and moon. Shown here is a rawhide shield housed at the British Museum in London.

American Indian artist George Catlin visited the Pawnees in the early 1830s and painted many portraits of Pawnee warriors, including this one entitled "Ill-Natured Man, a Skidi (Wolf) Pawnee."

Much of George Catlin's work is on display at the Smithsonian American Art Museum in Washington, D.C., including this portraiture of Big Elk, a Skidi (Wolf) chief.

This painting by Jacques Victor Eugene Froment-Delormel, which is on display at the Musee du Nouveau Monde, La Rochelle, France, depicts a Pawnee warrior in the wilderness. Froment-Delormel never visited the United States but was greatly influenced by George Catlin's work.

This buffalo hide painting depicts a 1720 battle between the Spanish and a combined force of Pawnee and Oto warriors and their French allies near present-day Schuyler, Nebraska. The Spanish force, which was led by Pedro de Villasur, had traveled to Nebraska on a reconnaissance mission to gather information on the French, but after they were defeated, the Spanish would never again reach this area of the Great Plains.

Renowned western artist and photographer William Henry Jackson traveled through Nebraska in the mid-1860s and painted this rendition of a Pawnee village, which includes several earth lodges.

turn back any American explorers or settlers coming into the disputed lands.

Within days after Malgares' visit, Zebulon Pike encountered the Pawnees. He had only a small band of nineteen men and was not in a position to impress the tribe with American might. The Pawnee chief Sharitarish told Pike to turn back. If he did not turn back on his own, Chief Sharitarish threatened, his people would turn him back themselves. Pike brazenly refused to back down. Disconcerted by this unexpected show of foolish bravery, they let him pass.

Pike and his men followed the trail of Malgares. Losing him, they then stumbled into Spanish territory and were made

Bicentennial. They see the celebrations as a way to celebrate their culture while promoting tourism.

Chris Howell, who lives in Kansas City, Kansas, is one such important promoter—he is the vice chairman of the Kansas Lewis and Clark Bicentennial Commission, in charge of coordinating events in the state depicting and celebrating the explorers' journey that officially began in May 1804, and lasted through 1806. He is one of the people who is making sure that every Indian tribe that lived anywhere near the path that Lewis and Clark took on their journey through Kansas is being properly recognized. He was also one of the Native people in the "Circle of Tribal Advisors," especially chosen to ensure that such activities as historical reenactments and opening ceremonies would accurately represent the nearly thirty Indian tribes encountered by Lewis and Clark. Such sensitivity by non-Indians, and such participation by Native Americans, reveals that much progress has been made on both sides of the historical fence. For more on the tribes Lewis and Clark encountered during their travels, go to *http://www.nationalgeographic.com/lewisandclark/record_tribes_016_4_17.html.*

prisoners of war. For four months, Zebulon Pike and his band were held in Chihuahua, but his being detained turned out to be a boon to American intelligence, for upon his release in 1807, Pike gave the U.S. government a detailed account of Spanish military positions, commanders, and other useful strategic information.

Other visitors to Pawnee territory were thirsty not for gold or the thrill of discovery but to spread the word of God. Missionaries, sometimes called "Black Robes," invaded the lands of the Pawnees on an errand of a spiritual nature. While the Pawnee people had Tirawa and other lesser gods, the missionaries brought them a new, all-powerful God, one of fire and brimstone and omnipotence.

The missionaries not only taught a faith; they changed the lives of countless Native Americans forever. Before they could accept and internalize the teachings of this new God, the Pawnees had to betray their ancestry and culture and become like white people. One Pawnee in particular whose life was affected by the new explorers and their beliefs was Knife Chief. In 1817, he met with William Clark, who had been named superintendent of Indian affairs and was residing in St. Louis. Clark impressed upon Knife Chief the great numbers of white people who would be coming, white people whose beliefs were very different from those of the Pawnees. Knife Chief and his son, Man Chief (or Petalesharro, as he is sometimes called), became increasingly troubled by the sacrificial rites of the Morning Star Ceremony. Finally, Man Chief took action to end the practice. In a dramatic gesture that is now a story of legendary proportions, on the dawn of the Morning Star Ceremony in 1817, Man Chief rode through a crowd of more than four hundred warriors and cut the elk-skin-bound Sioux girl Haxti from the scaffold at the critical moment, gave her a horse, and let her return to her people unharmed. Because of Petalesharro's efforts, human sacrifice was eliminated from the Morning Star Ceremony. A painting

The Pawnees first encountered non-Native people in the mid-sixteenth century, when Spain's Francisco Vásquez de Coronado traveled to present-day Kansas. However, with the exception of their dealings with French fur trappers, the Pawnees did not have much contact with whites until the early 1800s. This painting by Stephen Seymour depicts a treaty council between the U.S. Army and the Pawnees in 1819, shortly after the Pawnees signed their first treaty with the U.S. government.

of Petalesharro, made when he visited Washington, D.C., to receive a medal for his bravery, now hangs in an art gallery in Tuscaloosa, Alabama.

When white trappers began to invade the western mountains in the 1820s, they realized that the land was actually a far cry from what Lewis and Clark had called "the Great American Desert." One trapper in particular by the name of Jedediah Smith wound up in the area that is now Republic, Kansas, and wintered with the Pawnees there in 1825. When he returned, his vivid descriptions told of inexhaustible supplies of game, timber, and land; this encouraged others to come.

The Pawnees at first agreed to allow these new settlers to pass through. They had already signed a peace treaty with the

U.S. government to this effect in 1818. It was when the people lingered, forcibly taking the Pawnee land and its wealth, that real troubles began.

The dawn of the Industrial Revolution was the beginning of the Pawnees' darkest night. European technological advances made themselves apparent in Pawnee lands. By the mid-nineteenth century, telegraph lines spread across the plains like a great spider web. The white man began to survey and lay track for the train the Indians called the "iron horse" to travel upon. No formal treaties were signed establishing the railroads' right-of-way. Some of the lands the tracks crossed were those of the Pawnees, and Native American anxiety began to turn to outright rancor against the alien invaders.

On one morning in 1842, one hundred settlers in eighteen covered wagons left Independence, Missouri, and began the first crossing of the plains by settlers. The next year and every year after that the trickle of wagons increased to tidal wave proportions.

In the earliest days of the invasion into and through what was then called Indian country, some settlers were rather dismayed to cross the entire continent without having spotted an Indian. Many of the settlers on the wagon trains of the 1840s only saw Indians when they passed by trading posts or forts along the way. By 1847, there were three main trails leading to the Far West: the Santa Fe, Oregon, and Mormon. The Santa Fe Trail was first worn down by the travois, having had its beginnings as a trading and hunting route. The Mormon Trail was begun by the followers of Brigham Young, who led his people to what is now Salt Lake City, Utah. In addition to the three major trails, the Missouri River, fed by the Platte, provided transportation for traders and settlers via steamboat.

By this time, the Pawnees probably thought they had witnessed as large a migration of white people as was possible. Then, in 1848, the discovery of a precious yellow metal further west led to even more disruption of the Pawnee way of life. The discovery of gold in California in 1848 started a great transcontinental migration of miners, settlers, and others wanting to take advantage of the booming economy to be found in the West. The following year, wagons rolled across the plains as far as the eye could see. Along the Platte, where much of this activity occurred, buffalo became more wary. They avoided the noisy throngs of progress, eventually dividing themselves into two herds on the north and south sides of the river.

It was inevitable that the two cultures would clash. Settlers and other non-Indians held one of two opinions about Native Americans, both of which had their roots in paternalistic European attitudes. One belief was that the Indian was a proud, simple "child of nature," unencumbered by civilization and its immorality. The other view held that Indians were treacherous, bloodthirsty savages whose removal was necessary for the safety of the "civilized" world.

While both views were skewed, the policies of the U.S. government toward America's Native inhabitants were equally misguided. The establishment of a special organization to handle Indian affairs did little to improve the situation. Originally part of the U.S. Department of the Interior, the *Bureau of Indian Affairs* was established by the U.S. government in 1824. Its original purpose was "to safeguard the welfare of American Indians . . . act as trustee for tribal lands and funds, supervise the reservations and provide welfare and education facilities." However, Native Americans did not want or need to be protected.

The great overland migration of the nineteenth century brought more than people into Pawnee territory; white settlers and traders brought with them terrible diseases to which the Pawnees had no natural immunities. In 1831, the Pawnees were hit with their first major epidemic brought by white settlers. Smallpox, an infectious disease causing fever, headache, and festering sores, resulted in the deaths of more than half the Pawnee population. In 1849, cholera, a waterborne bacterial disease, became an epidemic and killed nearly half of what remained of the Pawnee population. The symptoms of cholera came on quickly, with severe diarrhea, dehydration, shock, and then death. Often, survivors were so frightened of cholera that they refused to bury the dead. Measles and tuberculosis also swept through the tribes, leaving death in their wake.

So weakened and dispirited were the Pawnees that by 1859, when they were ordered by the U.S. government to move to a reservation along the Loup River, near what is now Genoa, Nebraska, they went without a fight. They found no peace there, however. The longtime enemy of the Pawnees, the Sioux, went unchecked by the federal government, which the Pawnees thought would protect them. Bands of Sioux raided Pawnee villages, killing even more of the people. In August 1873, the Sioux attacked a Pawnee hunting band in a canyon near Trenton, Nebraska, killing almost everyone (today, the place is known as Massacre Canyon). To make matters worse, a series of severe droughts killed the verdant grasses upon which the buffalo fed, causing the great herds to migrate farther in search of food. Grasshoppers, which darkened the plains from horizon to horizon with their great numbers, destroyed what was left of the Pawnees' crops.

The Pawnees found themselves living a nightmare from which they could not awake. In 1876, they were forced to cede their Nebraska reservation—their traditional hunting grounds—to the U.S. government and migrate to Oklahoma.

As late as the mid-1800s, the great herds of buffalo upon which the Pawnees depended were almost too numerous to count. Estimates of the buffalo population by early explorers ranged from 20 to 60 million; one account mentions a horseback rider who traveled from sunrise to sunset through the same herd. There were several factors that led to the demise of the buffalo. Hunters and fur traders, the railroad, ranchers, and other settlers all played their parts in the extermination of the bison.

Certain parts of the buffalo, such as the tongue, were considered delicacies in Europe; the meat of the female buffalo was

Like all Plains Indians, the Pawnees' life largely revolved around the buffalo, but by the 1870s the buffalo were largely exterminated from the southern plains. In 1870 alone, 2 million buffalo hides were taken from Kansas and Nebraska. This 1874 photo, taken in Dodge City, Kansas, shows a large number of buffalo hides that are being prepared to be processed and shipped east.

especially tender. Hunters began the wanton slaughter of the bison to supply this new demand. Because they mostly killed the cows, the numbers of newborn buffalo calves grew smaller every spring. The demand for hides skyrocketed when a German furrier developed a tanning method to make buffalo hide extremely soft. As a result, an increasing number of fur traders sought their fortunes on the plains.

The results were tragically predictable. Pawnee hunting parties would come upon dead buffalo left to rot in the sun, with only the tongues, humps, and hides removed. Starvation began to be the rule rather than the exception in Pawnee life. The railroad also caused problems for the buffalo population. Settlers shot at the herds from their train cars just to watch the great beasts stagger and fall. It became a sport—something to pass the time while crossing the plains.

By 1878, the southern herd was wiped out except for a few small, isolated groups. The northern herd, whose migration route was cut off by ranchers who had begun to use barbed wire in 1874, succumbed to the rifles of the huntsmen shortly thereafter. The symbol of Pawnee freedom and culture was disappearing before their eyes. Then came what seemed to be a chance for the Pawnees to better themselves and perhaps change their destiny.

Across the plains, the Sioux were wreaking havoc with the U.S. government's plans to settle the country. Forgetful that they themselves had caused the insurrection by reneging on treaties, the federal government decided to put down the massive Sioux uprising. The U.S. government asked the Pawnees to help.

In 1864, the Civil War was still raging, and the Sioux were taking advantage of the fact that Union troops were busy fighting the Confederacy. There was little help for the settlers and other whites who roamed the plains. After losing thousands of lives and after futile attempts to control the Sioux through normal governmental controls, approximately two hundred Pawnees were made U.S. Army scouts, to serve in the Sioux Campaign of 1864 under Major Frank North and his brother, Captain Luther North.

The Pawnees must have seen this as an opportunity for revenge upon the Sioux Nation. Recent attacks by the Sioux were still fresh in Pawnee minds. To serve the new government with compensation *and* to strike a blow against their longtime enemies seemed a golden opportunity. In what is now termed "the Sioux Campaign," the company of Pawnee Scouts served alongside regular U.S. Army troops and fought with dauntless courage. Major Frank North became so popular with the Pawnee Scouts that they came to call him *Pani Leshar*, which means "Pawnee Chief."

Many Pawnee warriors joined the U.S. Army in the 1860s and '70s to serve as scouts to track down the Sioux and Cheyennes, first during the Sioux Campaign of 1864 and later to protect workers who were constructing the Transcontinental Railroad. Shown here are four Pawnee Scouts in 1869.

The scouts did so well in the Sioux Campaign that in 1867 they were again asked to aid the U.S. government by protecting construction workers on the Union Pacific Railroad. The completion of the first transcontinental railroad would unite the country, and Pawnee involvement in protecting the railroad was a terrible irony, for the iron horse brought more settlers to the plains, helping to seal the fate of the Pawnee and other tribes.

The Pawnees were chosen for this particular duty because the U.S. Army, most notably the soldiers of Fort Sedgwick, could not outfight the raiding war parties of the other tribes, all of whom were enemies of the Pawnee Nation. Since 1863, these war parties, composed of Sioux, Cheyenne, and Arapaho warriors, had been attacking the Union Pacific tracklayers and surveyors, taking lives, horses, and scalps. Colonel William Emory, the commander of Fort Sedgwick, was steadfastly opposed to "putting Cavalry uniforms on 200 half-wild Indians" and was offended that his superiors made this decision against his advice (he later admitted his error).

"Scouting" for Justice: What Happened to the Pawnee Scouts?

In 1989, the Pawnee Nation requested the repatriation of deceased Pawnee Indians and associated objects taken by the U.S. Army at Mulberry Creek, Kansas. The remains were those of six U.S. Army Pawnee Scout veterans, part of the original group who had been used by the U.S. government in both the Sioux Campaign and for the railroad-workers' protection during the 1860s and 1870s. These remains were first "collected" by U.S. Army personnel following a skirmish with these Indians, then turned over to the Army Medical Museum in Washington, D.C., before being sent to the Smithsonian Institution's Museum of Natural History.

One of the leaders in the fight for the Pawnee Nation's right to repatriate the remains for a proper burial was Walter Echo-Hawk. A senior attorney for the activist legal group Native American Rights Fund, he, along with NARF, filed a number of claims against the Smithsonian Institution in 1988. At the time, Echo-Hawk said, "The Smithsonian refused to deal with us," so NARF petitioned Congress to pass two acts of legislation to help the First Nations preserve their ancestors and their related objects. After fierce lobbying by NARF and the Pawnee Nation, Congress responded by passing the National Museum of the American Indian Act of 1989, which ultimately created the new museum by the same name. One of the stipulations in the NMAI Act was that the Smithsonian repatriate the scouts' remains, as well as other Native

Of all the interesting stories concerning this time in Pawnee history, one man's story stands out. A half-white, half-Pawnee man named James Murie was one of nine officers given charge of the two-hundred-strong contingent of scouts. Murie was made a captain of the cavalry because of his previous experience when, as second lieutenant, he led Pawnee scouts against the Sioux in what is now called the Powder River Expedition. He was given command of one of four companies in the new regrouped battalion.

James Murie had been raised by Pawnee foster parents on the reservation near Genoa, Nebraska. Perhaps one reason he

American remains, in the museum's vast collection. This act was followed closely by the second piece of legislation, the Native American Graves Protection and Repatriation Act (NAGPRA), which affects all other museums and archaeological archives in the United States.

Following the passage of the so-called "Smithsonian Law," the Pawnee Nation pursued its repatriation claims with the assistance of NARF attorneys and consultants James Riding In and Roger Echo-Hawk. Their efforts resulted in the repatriation and reburial of hundreds of deceased Pawnee Indians and tribal ancestors. Among these were the Pawnee Scouts, who were reburied with full ceremony by the tribe in 1995. With support and help from the U.S. Army, the scouts' remains were given a proper military escort from Washington, D.C., then buried with full military honors. Three tribes attended: the Pawnee, the Arikara, and the Wichita, because the reburial included other remains from these related tribes.

The scouts now rest in the Genoa City Cemetery in Genoa, Nebraska, on the old reservation lands that the Pawnees held before they were moved to Oklahoma. There are also about eight hundred more Pawnees who have been returned to the people for proper burial and subsequently reburied there. The Pawnee Nation has achieved similar victories from other museums since then.

accepted the assignment to protect the Union Pacific was because of a renegade Cheyenne named Turkey Leg. Not only were his Cheyenne bands harassing the Union Pacific tracklayers, Turkey Leg had also led a raid on the Genoa reservation in 1865, killing Murie's foster parents. The battalion was first issued Enfield rifles, then the more modern Spencer repeating rifles, which held seven rounds of ammunition in a tubular magazine and an eighth round in the chamber. The Spencers had a range of about six hundred yards. The scouts carried the Spencers in a carbine sling, which when not in use allowed the rifle to hang by the right hip, muzzle down, leaving the hands free.

The four companies were each assigned specific duties. One company guarded the survey crew; another the grading camp; a third the horse and mule herds. Murie's B Company was in charge of guarding the construction camp and the tracklayers. After the companies were in place, tracklayers were attacked by a band of approximately eight Sioux led by Red Cloud. The Sioux were ambushed by Murie's B Company before they got within range of the tracklayers. Then the Cheyenne attacked, led by the famous warrior Turkey Leg. Murie's forty Pawnees again repelled the raiders. Murie and his battalion of Pawnee Scouts helped to ensure peace long enough for the railroad to be completed.

The part the Pawnees played in helping white settlers establish roots in the West did little for them as a nation. The laws of the U.S. government would suppress them and all other Indian nations indiscriminately. In the end, all "red men" were treated in the same disgraceful way, whether they had been ally, guide, warrior, or scout in their previous dealings with the white man.

In the first half of the nineteenth century, the Pawnees had been on generally peaceful terms with the U.S. government. After that, however, U.S. government policy toward Native Americans in general seemed bent on assimilating the cultures and annihilating the histories of those who were here before.

James R. Murie (center, seated), who was the son of a Scottish-born U.S. Army captain, led a company of Pawnee Scouts during the Sioux-Cheyenne war of the 1860s. Photographed with Murie are Pawnee scouts Captain Jim and Billy Osborne (sitting), and John Buffalo, John Box, High Eagle, and Seeing Eagle (standing, left to right).

The *Major Crimes Act*, passed in 1885, dealt with the question of Native Americans who committed crimes against one another. The act provided that any Native American accused of a "major" crime, such as murder, came under the jurisdiction of the U.S. government. Without the consent of the Indian nations, their own judicial systems were rendered powerless, their sovereignty swept aside in blatant disregard.

In a seeming attempt to help Native Americans in the "assimilation" process, Congress passed the *Dawes Act* in 1887. Named after its sponsor, Massachusetts senator Henry L. Dawes, this act was also called the General Allotment Act, and served a twofold purpose. Dawes reasoned that Native Americans would be better able to fit in with mainstream

American culture if they owned land. The act allocated parcels of the existing reservations to individual male Native Americans; this was later changed to include females. The amount of land allotted depended upon one's age, marital status, and family condition (orphans under the age of eighteen received twice the land of children living with their parents, for example).

One problem with this idea was that, if Native Americans were given American citizenship and turned into landholders, they could also be taxed. To remove this burden, at least temporarily, Dawes included a twenty-five-year period in which the U.S. government would hold the allotted lands "in trust" for the allottees. This period ostensibly would allow Native Americans time to make a profit from farming the land. They could also move away and live in cities with non-Native Americans and learn how to make a living like the "average" American. The act provided for education and farming instruction toward these ends.

What white Americans failed to realize was that most Native Americans did not wish to learn farming the white man's way. In any case, much of the land given them for cultivation was barren wasteland. And when the act broke up reservation lands and gave Native Americans ownership of individual allotments, unscrupulous speculators could cajole individual Indians into selling their plots. Over time, the reservations would be eaten away piecemeal, and the land would be lost forever.

In their ignorance—or greed—lawmakers, politicians, settlers, and others concerned with "the Indian problem" praised Dawes for his genius. They saw his act as the perfect solution, which would "settle the Indian problem" once and for all. The act, however, completely destroyed the sovereignty of the Native American nations over their own people. Thanks to the Dawes Act, Native Americans found themselves owning less land than they had been allocated in the reservation treaties.

The remainder found its way into the hands of white settlers, and appeals to tribal courts meant nothing (one Native American historian has even said that these legislative acts and programs were set up with failure in mind. Former Alliance for Native American Indian Rights President Nick Mejia said in an interview, "The Indians were not supposed to survive, but to eventually perish. The European invasion was a disaster for the American Indian, since it compelled the Indian people to enter a cash economy, adopt different foods, and speak an alien language while divorcing the people from the land. Virtually every instance of communal stress can be traced to the shift from a land-based culture to one defined by 'consumerism' and a global economy.").

Native Americans were further humiliated as they began to lose their sense of belonging to a tribe. For seven centuries or more, Pawnee culture had as its cornerstone an attitude of interdependence, of belonging to each other. With each individual owning land, and with their communal properties dissolved, what had been the backbone of their social structure simply vanished.

After the Pawnees had lost virtually all their lands, another piece of legislation caused them to suffer even further. The *Curtis Act* of 1898 effectively abolished the rights of all tribal governments. The Pawnees were completely without power to rule, advise, educate, or lead their people, figuratively or otherwise. The people were completely and solely under the authority of the U.S. government.

Following the Curtis Act, in an effort to further "assimilate" or "Americanize" the Native American populations, Indian children were removed from their homes, often forcibly, and sent to school to learn the white man's ways (a popular government motto then was, "Kill the Indian—save the man."). After 1875, the Pawnee Industrial School was constructed near the Pawnee Indian Agency just outside Pawnee, Oklahoma. There, children were taught the white man's language, ways, and

After the Curtis Act was passed in 1898, many American Indians, including Pawnee children, a group of whom are pictured here at a reservation school on the Loup River in Nebraska in 1871, were taken from their homes and sent to school to be "Americanized." Pawnee children were not allowed to practice any of their customs or speak their language while at school.

beliefs. If a Pawnee child were caught doing anything reminiscent of the "old ways," he or she was often severely punished—often even beaten. It took more than three decades before the Curtis Act was invalidated.

The *Indian Reorganization Act* of 1934, or Indian New Deal, represented a turning point in federal Indian policy. Bureau of Indian Affairs Commissioner John Collier, whose efforts had inspired the legislation, was a man of unusual vision and a sense of fairness. During his tenure with the Bureau of Indian Affairs, he initiated sweeping reforms in Indian policies.

The Indian Reorganization Act had three basic tenets. The first one rescinded Dawes' allotment provisions, returning to the nations all lands not already sold to whites. Instead of the twenty-five-year trust agreement that Dawes had provided, the new act extended the trust period on allotments indefinitely. Collier had seen that when the twenty-five-year trust period ended, many Native Americans could still not pay the new taxes on their allotted lands and were forced to sell them, often to whites. This extension of the trust period thus protected the allottees and their lands.

The Indian Reorganization Act also set aside $2 million annually for the purpose of buying back lands previously sold to whites and returning them to the previous owners. There were also provisions for tribal reorganization, allowing the nations limited self-government similar to that of municipalities.

A third tenet in the Indian Reorganization Act held that qualified Native Americans would be appointed to various offices within the Bureau of Indian Affairs itself. Young, promising Indian students would be provided with loans for education from a $250,000 annual fund set aside for this purpose.

Originally, Congress passed the bill with the stipulation that Native American tribes in Oklahoma and Alaska should be excluded; they reasoned that these tribes, the Pawnee among them, were already being cared for and did not need the protection this legislation provided. But because of Collier's persistence, in 1936 Congress passed the Oklahoma Indian Welfare Act, which extended many provisions of the Indian Reorganization Act to Native Americans on reservations there.

The Pawnee Indian tribe of Oklahoma first ratified its constitution in 1938, following passage of the Oklahoma Indian Welfare Act of 1936. Following this, Native Americans, with a vision of having more say in their lives, established the National Congress of American Indians (NCAI). Founded in 1944 in Washington, D.C., the NCAI's mission was to "inform the public and federal government on tribal self-government, treaty rights, and a broad range of federal policy issues affecting tribal governments."

Congress also founded the Indian Arts and Crafts Board to improve the economic conditions of Native Americans by helping them showcase and sell Native handicrafts. The Indian Arts and Crafts Board, which is a part of the U.S. Department of the Interior, was created by Congress in order to promote the economic development of American Indians and Alaska Natives by expanding the Indian arts and crafts market. The board also administers a number of museums, whose gift shops offer authentic Native American crafts, and in October 2004, published a catalog of Native American artisans who have their work commercially available. The Indian Arts and Crafts Board—the only federal agency solely concerned with benefiting Native American cultural development—is committed to enforcing the Indian Arts and Crafts Act of 1990, which provides criminal and civil penalties for anyone selling or advertising products as "Indian-made" when they are not, thereby protecting the arts and crafts market share for all Native people. Using this legislation and new venues to sell their arts and crafts, an increasing number of Pawnee handmade crafts are now sold via the Internet, on and off the reservation, in shops, and in catalogs.

The twentieth century has seen further improvements in U.S. federal policy as it relates to the Pawnees. Feeling a sense of pride and perhaps also encouraged by a turning tide in "mainstream" American sentiments toward them, in 1946 the Pawnee tribe first gathered to celebrate the returning Pawnee veterans of World War II. Other positive changes were made as well. In 1957, reservation lands that had not been given to white settlers in Oklahoma were returned to the Pawnee people. In 1968, the Pawnee Nation regained ownership of some of the land that originally made up its Oklahoma reservation, which the U.S. government had granted them in an earlier treaty in exchange for their Nebraska hunting grounds.

Recently, during the end of the twentieth century and the beginning of the twenty-first, the Pawnees have begun to prosper, and even though the tribe can still see problems and feel despair, as in days of old they can look to the sky, see that with every darkness there is a dawn, and hope for a brighter future. Beginning in the 1970s and into the early twenty-first century, a new, promising season of change was upon the "People of the Stars."

4

The Modern Pawnee Nation

Today, a growing, progressive community exists on the 28,000-acres of Pawnee tribal land that comprises most of Pawnee County, Oklahoma. The Pawnee Nation, which is approximately 458 square miles, is located just outside the city of Pawnee in northeastern Oklahoma; of these individually owned lands, 686 acres are owned by the Pawnee Nation itself. From a nation that was almost wiped out, the tribe has grown to include more than three thousand *enrolled* members, and the land held by the Pawnees has expanded and is now spread out over a three-county area. Land use is mostly agricultural, with some oil and gas production.

Now, in the early twenty-first century, winds of change are beginning to blow in the Pawnee Nation. Due to the influence of more visionary non-Natives, and to the insistence of Native peoples, the Pawnees are now able to practice many of the rites and traditions nearly lost to them—but it was inevitable that the Pawnees would be

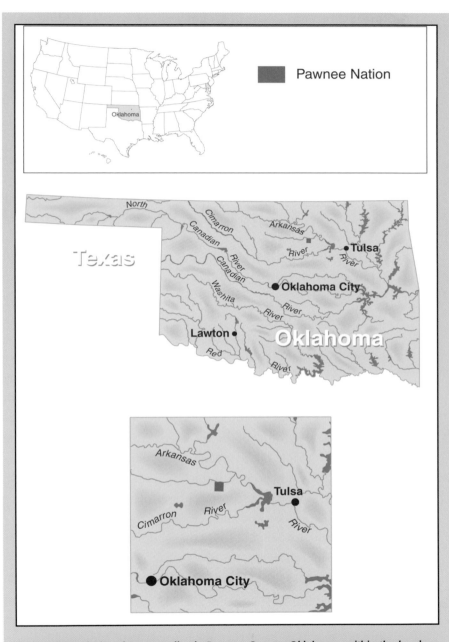

Today, the majority of Pawnees live in Pawnee County, Oklahoma, within the borders of the Pawnee Nation. According to the 2000 U.S. Census, there were approximately 2,500 Pawnees (belonging to one tribe), most of whom live in Oklahoma.

affected by their exposure to other cultures. For example, serving in the U.S. military, many young Pawnees were introduced
to new ways of thinking, and decided against returning to the
Pawnee Nation, believing that there was a better life for them
elsewhere. Since the 1970s, however, there has been a renewed
interest in the old ways and a longing for the sense of community that the people once shared.

The Pawnee Constitution, first adopted in 1938, was
amended in 1982 and again in 1997 and 2003. One of the first
changes the constitution adopted was to officially change the
name of the tribe from "Pawnee Tribe" to "Pawnee Nation of
Oklahoma"; a more recent constitutional amendment has
changed the requirement of blood quantum from 1/4 to 1/8 to
be listed as an official member of the Pawnee Nation. Dawna
Hare, executive assistant to President Howell, made these additional comments in an interview: "When the constitution was
established in 1938, it was the standard BIA boiler-plate constitution that many tribes were given, with one exception. We
have two councils: the Pawnee Business Council and the
Nasharo Council (see more on these, below). The problem with
those [early] constitutions is that the U.S. government developed these constitutions without giving any thought on the
manner in which [Native Americans] had been ruling themselves and the customs of the tribe. That is why many believe
that tribes have struggled: they were forced to adopt a way of
doing business that was alien to them."

The tribal government is made up of the eight-member
Pawnee Tribal Business Council, the superior governing body (it
is more commonly known as the Pawnee Business Council).
The former president of the Pawnee Nation is George Elton
Howell, who was replaced in 2005 by former Vice President
Ronald Rice. The new vice president is Pete Moore, who won
more than 38 percent of the popular vote in the May 7, 2005,
election. Council members are elected every four years in a general tribal election. Various committees appointed by the

Pawnee Business Council include committees on education, *repatriation*, health, budget and finance, culture and language, enrollment, property, library, and grievance. Commissions appointed by the Pawnee Business Council include the tax commission, gaming commission, environmental protection commission, utility commission, tribal development corporation, tribal employment rights office, and a housing authority. The Executive Office of the Pawnee Nation is in charge of directing and coordinating administrative activities for the tribe and oversees day-to-day operations. The executive office works in conjunction with the business council, developing agendas for and conducting research on items for council meetings, and assists in communicating important tribal information.

The other governing body is the Nasharo Council, also known as the chief council. Rather than being ruled by one chief, the Nasharo Council comprises eight traditional chiefs, with two chiefs representing each of the four bands. They are elected by their respective bands and serve four-year terms. The Nasharo Council membership predominantly consists of elders whose wisdom and advice is respected in the tribe, which is in keeping with the traditional values of the Pawnees, who hold elders in high esteem. The Nasharo Council has the right to review all acts of the Pawnee Business Council regarding membership and claims or rights resulting from treaties between the Pawnee Nation and the United States.

The Pawnee flag symbolizes their history and regained cultural pride. The field has a blue background with miniature stars and stripes, representing the United States. In the center is the head of a wolf (many of the Plains tribes called the Pawnees "wolves" because of their courage and cunning). Underneath the wolf's head are eight arrowheads. They symbolize the eight major wars in which the Pawnees served—the Indian Wars, the Spanish-American War, the two world wars, the Korean War, the Vietnam War, Desert Storm, and the war in Iraq.

The staff of the flag is a real warrior's lance, complete with flint spearhead. The staff is decorated with beadwork mounted on buckskin. The beads are multicolored, symbolizing those who have come before. At the top of the flag are four eagle feathers, representing the four Pawnee bands. Because cedar is a sacred token of prayer and peace, on special occasions a sprig is attached to the top of the Pawnee flagstaff. For additional information on the Pawnee flag, one may go to *http://www.pawneenation.org/flag.htm.*

Off tribal lands, the National Congress of American Indians, mentioned in the previous chapter, has grown since its inception in 1944 to include more than 250 tribal governments from every region in the country, and today is the oldest and largest tribal government organization in the nation. The NCAI also allows individual memberships, and encourages its members to be proactive by helping to contact Congress and federal government agencies about issues of concern to Native people. The Pawnee Nation has been a longtime member of the NCAI.

Within the Pawnee Nation, the Bureau of Indian Affairs and the Pawnee Tribal Administration and Programs offices are still housed in what used to be the boarding school (which is now registered as a Historic District), but something much more visionary has also taken up residence there. The Pawnee Industrial School, established in 1875, was a place of bad memories for many Pawnee ancestors, a place where they were forced to become more like "mainstream" Americans and beaten for clinging to the old ways and traditions. In 2004, President Howell continued a grass-roots effort to create a first-of-its-kind school within the old school's walls. Named the Pawnee Nation Academy, the old school's girl's dorm and dining hall were renovated and upgraded for use by high school *and* college students. The school opened its doors in the fall of 2005, and students at PNA take courses for high school credit, college credit, or certification licensing in special training. In early 2004, in an open letter to all the Pawnee people, President Howell wrote, ". . . so many of us had relatives who attended or worked at the former boarding school. When once the school's primary function was to assimilate Indian children into 'mainstream' society, the Academy's contemporary goal is to empower students to cross the threshold from potential to fulfillment." Today, the Pawnee Nation Academy encourages all students to celebrate their diversity and offers courses to anyone, tribal or not, who wants to learn. There are four major courses of study, including courses in engineering and construction, health and human services, business and marketing (including computer technology), and American Indian studies. Students who complete an area of study receive a program diploma; high school students may earn credits toward their high school diploma, and adult students receive college credit or certification in a specific licensing area.

The Pawnee Nation has grown to include a community building, a tribal trading post, a wellness center, a fire station, a family development center, and a travel plaza. The trading post sells what you might normally find in a small grocery, as well as Native American handicrafts. The wellness center operates through a partnership with the Pawnee Nation, Pawnee Public Schools, the city of Pawnee and the Pawnee County Commission, and provides a gymnasium for the high school basketball teams. The travel plaza is located eight miles south of Pawnee on the Cimarron Turnpike, and also serves as a truck stop, with a sandwich shop and convenience items inside. Modeled after the traditional earth lodge, the roundhouse is used by the Pawnee community for special tribal functions and gatherings. A new health center, built by the Pawnee Nation for Indian Health Services under the auspices of Public Law 93-638, was completed in March 2004. The health center has a staff of more than 140 people and has a physical therapy department, a dental facility, and is offering more specialized services than the previous, outdated facility.

Like many other nations, the Pawnee has a gaming enterprise. Located in the Pawnee Nation Casino and Trading Post on Agency Road, the gaming enterprise is managed by the Pawnee Tribal Development Corporation, and the profits go toward the welfare, health, and safety of the Pawnee people. The Pawnee Tribal Development Corporation is the economic-development arm of the Pawnee Nation. It serves to protect the tribe's assets while giving the tribe a kind of "firewall" to do business in the best interest of the Pawnee people (many businesses will not work with tribes without this mechanism for collecting debts or settling business matters, because tribes, like other governments, have sovereign immunity). In January 2005, the Pawnee Nation entered into an agreement with Lake Entertainment, Inc., a company that helps in the development and management of casinos, many of which are tribal-owned. Plans are now being made to expand the gaming facilities to three separate casino resorts, the largest of which will have a hotel and golf course as part of its complex.

Gaming brings both opportunities and challenges for the Pawnee Nation. There are some people who oppose gaming, but according to reports from the president's office, these individuals are in the minority. In a written statement from executive headquarters, Dawna Hare, executive assistant to then-President George Howell wrote: "We are so new in gaming that it is difficult to say [if it has caused problems of any significance]. Gaming must be used as a vehicle to develop a diversified economy. It has brought our people jobs that they did not have previously and our little gaming facility/trading post has provided a gathering place for many of us. Many of our members patronize the establishment and feel very comfortable there. We feel a sense of ownership." In addition to the new businesses springing up, there are a variety of churches both on and off tribal lands. The Methodist, Baptist, and Native American churches are represented, among others.

The Pawnee people wear traditional clothing at tribal

dances and powwows. Otherwise, their dress is much the same as that of any other American. Their diet consists of what you might eat every day, as well as some traditional foods such as corn soup, buffalo meat, blue corn mush, and fried bread.

The future for the Pawnee people is perhaps brighter now than it has been since the coming of white people. True, if one were to focus only on the negative aspects, it would seem that alcoholism, suicide, poverty, and a lack of opportunities are the overwhelming facts of twenty-first-century life. But these are people with vision and ambition, as were their ancestors before them. The Pawnees are working to change their lot, for the present and the future.

The Pawnee Health and Community Services Department has established special programs aimed at dealing with depression and suicide; another program they began in 1999 is called REACH 2010. The acronym stands for Racial and Ethnic Approaches to Community Health, and the goal of REACH 2010 is to reduce or entirely eliminate diseases such as diabetes and cardiovascular diseases by encouraging the people to become more physically active. The program, funded by the Centers for Disease Control in Atlanta, Georgia, works with the State of Oklahoma Health Department and seven other tribes, and offers such activities as archery, ballet, karate, swimming, and basketball. The substance abuse program provides education, referral, prevention activities, counseling, and aftercare to individuals and their affected families, and also offers use of a new fitness center, complete with a child-care center, which opened in January 2005 to all participants. As with many other tribal programs, the substance abuse program is not only open to Indians and non-Indians but serves the entire community.

To care for the elderly who are unable to cook or feed themselves, the Elderly Meals Program was developed. The tribe also runs the Indian Children Welfare Program, which is supported by funds from the Pawnees and by volunteer efforts.

Under the visionary guidance of President Howell, the

Pawnees worked to develop an Indian-owned and managed radio station, featuring Indian-related entertainment and news content. The people are working to establish an annual film festival, which is to be based in an old movie theater in downtown Pawnee and will highlight student-made productions, and a new construction company will soon be part of the economic growth within the Pawnee Nation.

Another unique problem that Native Americans have is the struggle of obtaining their ancestors' remains. Renewed pride in their heritage has encouraged the Pawnees to try to reclaim their ancestors, the remains of which are currently on display in museums and private collections both here and abroad. Many of these were dug by "treasure hunters" making their fortunes through modern-day grave robbing. The Pawnee Tribal Business Council has set up a repatriation committee, which, as the name implies, sees to the proper burial of the recovered remains of their ancestors. Many artifacts, too, which are traded or are in public or private collections are eligible to be repatriated.

The door to the future is wide open for Pawnee children. All Pawnee students showing promise are eligible for funds to attend college or to get vocational training. Many tribal members have become attorneys, doctors, nurses, teachers, and other professionals. The Pawnee Education Department and Indian Education Committee have established special tutorial programs to enhance not only higher education but also cultural awareness for Pawnee students. Beginning in the 1990s, the Pawnee Business Council urged the Pawnee Public School to offer Pawnee language classes. Under Oklahoma House Bill 1017, these classes meet the foreign language requirement, and today Pawnee language classes are open to all interested students in the school system. The course has been implemented in all grades beginning with kindergarten through twelfth grade, and uses not only interactive computer tutorials but also an instructor/facilitator. Another way the Pawnees are preserving

The Pawnee Indian Village State Historic Site and Interpretive Center near Courtland, Kansas, was built to preserve the site of an 1820s Pawnee village that was once home to more than two thousand Pawnees. Shown here is the outline of two of the earth lodges in the late 1960s, prior to the construction of the museum.

and protecting their language and their culture is with the help of elders: Through the years, in an effort to save their oral histories and traditions, the stories of elder Pawnees have been and continue to be recorded before they are lost to time.

Public tours of the Pawnee Nation are currently in the planning stages, but children from nearby schools often visit and attend dances and ceremonies held at the tribal campgrounds. There are two museums of note that seek to preserve the memory of a people who once freely roamed the plains and called it home. Near Courtland, Kansas, lies the Pawnee Indian Village State Historic Site and Interpretive Center. The building, a museum, was built in the shape of an earth lodge. The site for the museum near the Republican River was the natural choice; an ancient grouping of earth lodges, storage pits, and a wall were uncovered there in the mid-1900s, and the site remains the only major intact Pawnee village site. State historians, anthropologists, and archaeologists all agree that this was the place where Jedediah Smith, the American trapper, wintered with the Pawnees in 1826, and it is believed that this was also the site where Zebulon Pike visited with the Pawnees. Although the museum was closed for a few months during 2004 due to tornado damage, it was renovated and reopened in January 2005. The museum itself was constructed around the excavated floor of one of the larger earth lodges, and items found during the excavation have been replaced in the same spot in which they were discovered. Also on display is a medicine bundle worn by a small girl who survived the Sioux attack at Massacre Canyon. It has been passed down through the generations, and descendants of the surviving girl donated the bundle to the museum in 1987.

South of Anadarko, Oklahoma, Indian City USA has exhibits depicting the life of the Pawnee and six other tribes. This living-history museum provides an accurate sampling of how these tribes lived, and there is an excellent outdoor, full-sized replica of a Pawnee earth lodge that is complete in every detail, because Pawnee elders were used as advisors in the project. There is also a rather large buffalo herd on adjoining acreage, and Native American dances and powwows are held throughout the year.

For the people of the Pawnee Nation, perhaps the greatest challenge for preserving their culture lies within themselves. In a world that denigrates the unique and places greater value on cultural assimilation, they must strive to maintain their spiritual integrity and cultural heritage.

More than a few Pawnees have brought honor to themselves and their people with their special talents. Brummett

Larry EchoHawk, who was the first American Indian to hold the office of state attorney general—a position he held in Idaho from 1990 to 1994—is currently a tenured professor at the J. Reuben Clark School of Law at Brigham Young University. EchoHawk was also the Democratic nominee for governor of Idaho in 1994 and served on the Democratic National Committee from 1994 to 1997.

Echohawk, a writer and artist living in Tulsa, Oklahoma, designed the flag for the nation and his wife, Terry, is a published author. His nephew, Larry EchoHawk, is a former attorney general of Idaho and in 1994 became the U.S. Democratic Party candidate for governor of that state, raising speculation that he could be the first Native American to hold gubernatorial office in U.S. history (he was defeated by Phil Batt in

Walter Echo-Hawk (speaking), a senior staff attorney for the Native American Rights Fund in Boulder, Colorado, was instrumental in helping to pass repatriation legislation—both the National Museum of the American Indian Act (1989) and the Native American Graves Protection and Repatriation Act (1990)—that called for the return of American Indian remains and cultural items from museums.

1994). Writer Anna Lee Walters has published many stories of Pawnee life, preserving in print what otherwise might have been lost forever. She is also the director of the Navajo Community Press in Tsaile, Arizona.

Other Pawnee people have achieved success in the areas of activism and legislation. The media attention garnered by such efforts as repatriation of Native American remains has caused more Native American people to speak up, be more assertive, and address sensitive issues, such as the ownership and proper burial of their ancestors and related artifacts. John Echohawk, executive director of the previously mentioned Native American Rights Fund, put his law degree to use by establishing NARF in 1977. NARF provides legal aid to tribes and individual Native Americans, to ensure that their basic human rights are protected in the courts. His cousin, Walter Echo-Hawk, is a senior attorney with NARF, and was an advocate for the Native American Graves Protection and Repatriation Act of 1989 (NAGPRA). (For more information on NAGPRA and repatriation issues, see the sidebar on page 64, "What Happened to the Pawnee Scouts?").

Perhaps the most significant sign that times are really changing for the better for the Pawnees, and all Native American people, has been the opening of the National Museum of the American Indian (NMAI) in Washington, D.C. Opened by the Smithsonian Institution in September 2004 at a cost of $199 million, the museum is located on a 4.25-acre site just east of the National Air and Space Museum. After nearly fifteen years of planning and collaboration with tribal communities, the vision became a reality. The opening was celebrated with hundreds of visitors and Native American dignitaries (including three Pawnee Business Council members). Among the museum's artwork and artifacts is a collection entitled "Window on Collections: Many Hands, Many Voices." This exhibit features thousands of artifacts, including many from the free life on the Great Plains, such as beaded objects, peace medals, cradle boards, and weaponry. The museum is staffed predominantly by people of tribal affiliation, including several Pawnees, such as Thomas Evans, who is on the collections staff. He and other members of the collections staff have recorded and documented more than 335 items of Pawnee origin, including buffalo robes, weapons, gaming pieces, children's clothing, and more. Another priceless historical record is the museum's photo archives, containing approximately 160,000 images from daguerreotypes to digital images, all recording Native Americans and their culture.

Another significant sign of better times to come is the growing number of nonprofit organizations coming to the aid of Native Americans. One example is the American Indian

Kevin Gover, who served as assistant secretary for Indian Affairs under President William J. Clinton from 1996 to 2001, currently serves as professor of law and affiliate professor of the American Indian Studies Program at Arizona State University.

Education Foundation (AIEF). A member of National Relief Charities, the AIEF is one of the largest grantors of Native American college scholarships in the country, and provides such basics as school supplies and backpacks to younger students. AIEF is such a strong supporter of college-attending Native Americans that instead of the usual 20 percent retention rate among Native students, 91 percent of their scholarship-supported students continue their college education rather than dropping out.

Another tradition has been retained since the 1940s. Since first gathering to celebrate the returning Pawnee veterans of World War II (which was originally sponsored by World War I veterans), the celebration is now part of Pawnee tradition and has since become an annual event. The Pawnee Indian

Homecoming and Powwow is now a four-day event, held around the first weekend in July at the Pawnee Fairgrounds. Here participants enjoy traditional foods, dancing, various contests, softball games, and a parade. There is also a five-mile endurance race, named after Hawk Chief, a Pawnee scout who was the first person to run a mile in less than four minutes. He first set this record in the mid-1870s and it remained unbroken for eighty years, until Englishman Roger Bannister ran the mile in 3:59.4 in 1954.

In many ways the city of Pawnee celebrates its link with the tribe. It is the home of Pawnee Bill's Wild West Show, which entertains tourists with Native American warriors and dancers. A museum with artifacts of the "Old West," as well as endless parades and celebrations, are all reminders of the connection the town has with Pawnee culture.

On April 29, 1994, President Bill Clinton held the first Native American summit since 1822. He pledged "to respect tribal governments and improve relations between [his] administration and the Indians." He promised to "heal the pain" of the nations in various ways, one of which will be to consult with them on future federal Indian policies. Kevin Gover, himself a member of the Pawnee Nation and assistant secretary of the interior during the Clinton Administration, issued the first apology made to Indian nations for the wrongs done to them, and the failed governmental policies of the United States (Gover currently serves as a professor of law at Arizona State University—another example of a Pawnee making a significant contribution to Indian affairs). Although many Native Americans remain skeptical in light of similar overtures in the past, there is hope that at last the descendants of the people who were here before us will have a greater voice in governing their affairs. Since 1994, there has not been another Native American summit, and the promises President Clinton made remain unkept. However, there is a glimmer of hope. In 2004, President George W. Bush signed into law the American Indian

Probate Reform Act, authored by U.S. Senator Ben Nighthorse Campbell (Northern Cheyenne) and supported by Secretary of the Interior Gale Norton. This new law may finally facilitate the consolidation of Indian land ownership and is a major step for Indian trust reform.

Every civilization has periods of growth and decline. Perhaps after their long night in a valley of despair, the Pawnees are finally in sight of the mountaintop, where they will be close enough to touch the stars from whence they came.

The Pawnees at a Glance

Tribe	Pawnee
Culture Area	Great Plains
Geography	Present-day Kansas and Nebraska
Linguistic Family	Caddoan
Current Population (2000)	approximately 2,500
First European Contact	Francisco Vásquez de Coronado, Spanish, 1541
Federal Status	Recognized; tribal lands in northeastern Oklahoma

>13000 B.C.	The great Native American migration from Asia (predominant theory).
A.D. 1250	Pawnees migrate to the Great Plains from the southwestern part of this continent.
1541	Francisco Vásquez de Coronado explores the American territories then known as "New Spain" and meets the Pawnees, who obtain horses from the Spaniards; horses eventually become intrinsic to Plains life.
1803	The United States acquires 830,000 square miles of continental territory from Napoleon Bonaparte of France through the Louisiana Purchase.
1804–1806	Meriwether Lewis and William Clark, with their "Corps of Discovery," explore the West.
1806	American explorer Zebulon Pike and Spanish explorer Don Facundo Malgares travel the West, in what would today be termed as "intelligence-gathering" missions.
c. 1817	Man Chief, or Petalesharro, dramatically puts an end to the human sacrifice ritual called the "Morning Star Ceremony."
1818	The first treaty between the U.S. government and the Pawnee tribe is signed, allowing settlers to pass through Pawnee tribal lands (this is quickly abused by settlers).
1825	American trapper Jedediah Smith winters with the Pawnees; his tales of inexhaustible supplies of game, timber, and land encourage others to come to Pawnee territory.
1831	Pawnees are hit with the first major epidemic of smallpox, a disease carried by settlers and against which they have no immunity.
1840s	The "Great Emigration" of settlers into and through traditional Pawnee territory.
1848	Gold discovered in California, which leads to even greater traffic in Pawnee lands.
1849	Cholera kills half of the Pawnee population.

1859   Pawnees ordered to move to a reservation near what is now Genoa, Nebraska; dispirited, they do so.

1860s   Transcontinental Railroad constructed.

1860–1885   Buffalo herds dwindle to near extinction due to white man's slaughter and competition with settlers' herds for grazing lands.

1864   Pawnees agree to serve as U.S. Army scouts, first serving in the Sioux Campaign, then later (1867) protecting railroad workers from other tribes' attacks, especially the Sioux.

1873   Longtime enemies of the Pawnees, the Sioux, attack them in what is now known as Massacre Canyon, without protection promised by the U.S. government from such assaults.

1875   Pawnee Industrial School constructed near the Pawnee Indian Agency; Pawnee children are removed from their homes to learn white people's ways.

1876   Pawnees are forced to cede their Nebraska reservation and move to Oklahoma.

1885   Major Crimes Act renders Native American judicial system useless.

1887   General Allotment Act (Dawes Act), which allocates parcels of land to individual Pawnee people, with communal ownership of reservation land abolished. The tribe loses more of its previously agreed upon reservation acreage, which is lost to white settlers.

1898   Congress passes the Curtis Act, denying tribal governments sovereignty and places all Native Americans completely under the control of the U.S. government.

1924   U.S. grants Native Americans citizenship.

1934   Congress passes the Indian Reorganization Act, providing some relief to oppressed Native people, and is the beginning of attempts to protect tribal lands and recognize sovereign tribal governments. It excludes, however, those Natives in Oklahoma and Alaska—including the Pawnees.

1936 Native Americans deemed eligible for social security— including those in Oklahoma—through the Oklahoma Indian Welfare Act, which extends provisions of the IRA to those Native peoples.

1938 Pawnees ratify their constitution (amended in 1982, 1997, and 2003).

1944 National Congress of American Indians is founded in Washington, D.C. By the beginning of the twenty-first century, it is destined to become the oldest and largest tribal government organization in the nation and include more than 250 tribal governments.

1957 Reservation lands that have not been given to white settlers are returned to the Pawnees.

1968 The Pawnee Nation regains ownership of much of the land that made up its original Oklahoma reservation, previously granted to them in exchange for Nebraska hunting grounds.

1970 Native American Rights Fund, a watchdog-for-tribal-justice legal group, is founded in Boulder, Colorado.

1990 Indian Arts and Crafts Act is established in an effort to promote and protect Native cultural development and economics.

1990s Pawnee Public School offers Pawnee language and culture classes to all interested students.

2004 Census figures report 3,000 enrolled members of the Pawnee Nation; the Pawnee Nation is now 28,000-acres, with an established government, schools, and a vision for the future; National Museum of the American Indian opens in Washington, D.C.

2005   Pawnee Nation Academy established on the campus of the old Pawnee Industrial School, offering college courses and specialized training to members of the Pawnee Nation.

band—A loosely organized group of people who are bound together by the need for food and defense, by family ties, or by other common interests.

Bureau of Indian Affairs (BIA)—A U.S. government agency within the Department of the Interior. Originally intended to manage trade and other relations with Indians, the BIA now seeks to develop and implement programs that encourage Indians to manage their own affairs and to improve their educational opportunities and general social and economic well-being.

Caddoans—The ancestors of the Pawnees, who lived in the area immediately west of the Mississippi River.

cedar—A type of pine tree that has especially fragrant and durable wood. Cedar is a sacred substance to the Pawnees.

counting coup—Performing acts of valor during warfare; or, a system of ranking such acts.

Curtis Act—A federal law that placed Native Americans completely under the control of the U.S. government, denying them the right to govern themselves.

Dawes Act—Also known as the General Allotment Act, a federal law that divided tribal land holdings into small plots to be held as private property by individual Native Americans. The Dawes Act severely reduced the acreage held by Native Americans and undermined tribal traditions of communal land ownership.

earth lodge—A large, round dwelling made of support poles covered with a mix of mud, grass, and rocks and occupied during the spring and fall.

Hunt Police—A special society of Pawnee men who enforced certain rules surrounding the buffalo hunt that were designed to increase the hunt's success.

Indian Reorganization Act (IRA)—The 1934 federal law that ended the policy of allotting plots of land to individuals and encouraged the development of reservation communities. The act also provided for the creation of autonomous tribal governments.

Major Crimes Act—A federal law that placed any Native American who committed a serious crime under the jurisdiction of the U.S. court system, thereby undermining a tribe's ability to govern itself.

medicine bundle—A collection of sacred objects contained in a special carrying case. Among the Pawnees, certain bundles represent the creation, the four semi-cardinal directions, and intellectual creativity.

Morning Star Ceremony—A traditional Pawnee religious ceremony performed in the spring that involved the sacrifice of an adolescent girl from an enemy tribe.

repatriation—A returning of historically significant artifacts, ancestral human remains, and other objects to the tribes of origin by museums and other archaeologically interested groups.

shaman—A holy man, also known as a priest or medicine man, who advised the tribe and performed protective rites.

Sioux—A confederation of tribes that inhabit the northern Great Plains. The Sioux were traditionally considered enemies of the Pawnees.

sweat lodge—A special lodge that was heated and filled with steam for baths and purification rituals.

Books

Andrist, Ralph K. *Long Death: The Last Days of the Plains Indians.* New York: Collier Books, 1964.

Blaine, Martha Royce. *Pawnee Passage: 1870–1875.* Norman, Okla.: University of Oklahoma Press, 1990.

Cantor, George. *North American Indian Landmarks: A Traveler's Guide.* Detroit, Mich.: Visible Ink Press, 1993.

Capps, Benjamin. *The Great Chiefs.* Alexandria, Va.: Time-Life Books, 1975.

Creigh, Dorothy Weyer. *Nebraska: A Bicentennial History.* New York: Norton, 1977.

Davis, Kenneth S. *Kansas: A Bicentennial History.* New York: Norton, 1976.

Erdoes, Richard, and Alfonso Ortiz. *American Indian Myths and Legends.* New York: Pantheon Books, 1984.

Grinnell, George Bird. *Two Great Scouts and Their Pawnee Battalion: The Experiences of Frank J. North and Luther H. North, Pioneers in the Great West, 1856–1882, and Their Defence of the Building of the Union Pacific Railroad.* Lincoln, Nebr.: University of Nebraska Press, 1996.

Lankford, George E. *Native American Legends.* Little Rock, Ark.: August House, 1987.

McSpadden, J. Walker. *Indian Heroes.* New York: Thomas Y. Crowell, 1950.

Nathan, Adele. *The Building of the First Transcontinental Railroad.* New York: Random House, 1950.

Tassin, Ray. *Red Men in Blue.* Clinton, Mass.: Colonial Press, Inc., 1960.

Taylor, Colin F. *The Plains Indians.* Avenel, N.J.: Crescent Books, 1994.

Weltfish, Gene. *The Lost Universe: Pawnee Life and Culture.* Lincoln, Nebr.: University of Nebraska Press, 1977.

Websites

American Indian Education Foundation
www.aiefprograms.org

The National Museum of the American Indian
www.americanindian.si.edu

Aboriginal Multi-Media Society
(has more than 12,000 full-text articles with searchable archives)
www.ammsa.com

Indian Country Today
www.indiancountry.com

Native American News
www.indianz.com

InterTribal Bison Cooperative
www.intertribalbison.org

Pawnee Indian Village Museum
http://www.kshs.org/places/pawneeindian/history.htm

Native American Graves Protection and Repatriation Act
www.nagpra.org

Native American Rights Fund
www.narf.org

The Pawnee Nation's Official Website
www.pawneenation.org

Handbook of Texas Online: The Pawnee Indians
http://www.tsha.utexas.edu/handbook/online/articles/PP/bmp52.html

INDEX

PICTURE CREDITS

Theresa Jensen Lacey is author of more than seven hundred articles for newspapers and magazines, a contributor to Chicken Soup for the Soul books, and has published several other books, including *The Blackfeet* in the INDIANS OF NORTH AMERICA series. Lacey is of Cherokee and Comanche descent, a Charter Member of the National Museum of the American Indian, and a member of Western Writers of America. Lacey is also a teacher and has a master's degree in education. For more information on Lacey's work, access her website at *www.tjensenlacey.com.*

Ada E. Deer is the director of the American Indian Studies program at the University of Wisconsin–Madison. She was the first woman to serve as chair of her tribe, the Menominee Nation, the first woman to head the Bureau of Indian Affairs in the U.S. Department of the Interior, and the first American Indian woman to run for Congress and secretary of state of Wisconsin. Deer has also chaired the Native American Rights Fund, coordinated workshops to train American Indian women as leaders, and championed Indian participation in the Peace Corps. She holds degrees in social work from Wisconsin and Columbia.